W9-AFJ-750

Journey to Empowerment

Journey
to
Empowerment

MARIA D. DOWD

BET Publications, LLC
http://www.bet.com

NEW SPIRIT BOOKS are published by

BET Publications, LLC
c/o BET BOOKS
One BET Plaza
1900 W Place NE
Washington, DC 20018-1211

Library of Congress Card Catalogue Number: 2004101673
ISBN: 1-58314-494-3

First Printing: August 2004
10 9 8 7 6 5 4 3 2

Printed in the United States of America

This book is dedicated to my daughters, Janelle and Lauren, and to my mother "Miss Lula" for faithfully and lovingly serving in the capacity of *keeping it real*. Oh, how interesting the relationships between mothers and daughters can be. They take on dynamic lives of their own, as we try so hard to "not be like," yet through our journeys of self-awareness and rediscovery—and in our heart of hearts—we smile and thank God for our common denominators, as well as for the lessons taught, hard as some may be to swallow. And, I'm not just talking about mother-to-daughter lessons, but also those more gripping daughter-to-mother ones. Yes, my darlings Janellipooh and Ladybug, this is a tribute to the both of you.

I also want to acknowledge and thank the brother- and sisterfriends who have journeyed along with me, leaving extraordinary marks on my many lives and my Spirit—Brook, Chris, Dave, Donovan, Emily, Everett, Jamaal, Jan, Lyndon, Sis. Mary, Mutima, Nadine, Rhonda, Daddy Richard, Renee, Sandra, Sarah, Steve (especially for resurrecting my computer on this final deadline night!) . . . and, my beloved

Grandparents for paving the way. Tremendous hugs to the twenty thousand sistahs who supported African American Women on Tour over the past thirteen years. Each of you, my Earth Angels, has shown up just at the right time with just the right blessing . . . and wing span. Thank you for your love, genius, support and guidance. And, Astämari Batekun, you'll forever dwell in my heartspace. Jah love, light, and blessings. Hashima.

Finally, I thank God for bestowing such awe-inspiring gifts and the capacity to bring them to fruition.

Introduction

Journey to Empowerment offers readers a miscellany of life-transforming experiences and contemplations. It is a key that will hopefully unlock, touch, and liberate our spirits. Through the reflections of others who've walked in our shoes, I truly hope that you'll sashay into a brighter, more lighthearted place.

Journey to Empowerment would not *be* if not for the holy boldness of my collaborators who have generously bared their souls and truths with the world. I know it took wrestling with emotions and deep breaths to step out and share their moments of reckoning. As I read and pondered, I felt it; as I'm sure you will, too.

The added value of *Journey to Empowerment* is the unconditional permission that has been granted for *your* Spirit to speak its mind and move those thoughts into words. It's your turn. Yes, within these pages. You have unbridled permission to dream, journal, and mindlessly doodle . . . outside of the box of everyday existence. Write to clear your mind so that the heart can hear the truth and see the vision more clearly. In that quiet time and space, write and write . . . from the depths of your being. Don't mull over structure, grammar, or political correctness. Shake up your soul and revere in the enlightening experience. You may use the journal prompts provided, or you may not. Just do what YOUR heart desires. Allow your thoughts to flow, then bask. Permission granted. And, who knows. Your writings just may be the innards of our next *Journey to Empowerment* chapter.

    . . . Contemplate quietly,
      . . . Thank prayerfully,
        . . . Dream outrageously,
          . . . Speak honestly,
            . . . Process freely,
              . . . Act courageously,
                . . . Heal wholly,
                  . . . And live abundantly.

With love and laughter,
Maria

Journey to Community and Connectedness

No matter where we have been on our
Individual journeys on this earth or
Where we are going, We are One.

— Mary-Frances Winters

The Purpose Posse: Set on Due Course

BY MARIA DENISE DOWD

Our vessel is graced with tireless souls.
Determined in this soliloquy of life,
To stay on due course for the North Star.
Our collective energies crescendo,
In a sea-foam green kind of way.
Each season East meets West,
South heads North.
In b'twixt and b'tween, we stay on path.
While the high seas are rapturous,
They soon become tranquil.
Tropical, then cool; still, then breezy.
Through locks and twists, curls, and waves,
Our passion engulfs us in the sweetness
Of the grassroots cause and the empowering effects.
The navigator is on board, and so are the shipmates.
Collectively we set sail . . . on due course.

Purpose Posse

By Maria Denise Dowd

Once upon a time, I heard the term "Purpose Posse." Bertice Berry used it and it became a permanent part of my "people meditations." Those two words rang a chime in my head at a time when it was dizzy with fighting what I already knew in my heart. I had allowed too many of the wrong people into my space and they were wreaking havoc on *my* legs and my legacy. I was in a place where I was chasing after and running from, and getting nowhere fast. I had finally come to a realization—and goodness was it painful—that this absolutely crazy time and place was a direct reflection of my ill-fated attempt to sail my ship in directions that I knew wasn't right for me. My Spirit had leaks and those holes rendered my ability to listen to God's whispers impossible.

The comings and goings of men and women in our lives is not by random selection. The right people come into our lives at very specific times, for very specific reasons, as do the wrong people, if for no other reason than to prompt our internal Soul Purpose device and to nudge—or smack—us back onto our Divine right path. The wrong people teach us one valuable lesson—discernment. And, the truest test is on high seas. Who helps us sail through calm and stormy weather and uncharted courses? Who is there for the long haul, and who abandons us at the next port? Who feels like excess baggage? Who attempts to persuade us to debark before we've completed our journey? Who is so fear-filled they take flight or fight us to veer South, when our internal compass points North? Too often in our lives, we give rebels, pirates, and other mutinous spirits permission to embark. And, then we're forced to pay handsome ransoms for our liberation, our peace of mind.

Aside from that brief moment of insanity, my life continues to be blessed with many adoring, brilliant, innovative, authentic men and women who step onboard my vessel, bearing distinctive domestic and imported blends of soul-soothing and spirit-raising gifts. You know you're on purpose and with your Divine-right Purpose Posse when your heart is calm and your mind rides the waves with ease and grace. You know it because you feel it. And, you feel it because you've sealed the leaks and have allowed Spirit to guide you. Even when our "human-ness" surfaces and rears its "oogly" side, we're there when our hearts remain open, loving, forgiving, insightful, and faith-filled. Take a look around and take stock of the company you keep.

Keepers of Compassion wrap a thousand arms and thousand hearts around yours and understand from where you come, even when you don't understand yourself.

Keepers of Manhood are our brothers, fathers, uncles, and grandfathers who call for discipline, respect, and commitment to upholding family. They teach our boys and remind our men.

Keepers of Womanhood are our sisters, mothers, aunties, and grandmothers who call for responsibility, nurturing, and commitment to sustaining family. They teach our daughters and remind us.

Keepers of Spirituality and Healing Arts lay hands and help us to realign mind with body with spirit.

Keepers of the Compass are our logicians, our voices of reasoning and grounding. They check in to ensure that all things are on due course and according to schedule.

Keepers of the Rig and Cargo help to keep our cupboards stocked, our bodies able, and our environment safe and sound from encroaching winds and water.

Keepers of Codes of Conduct remind us of our relationship with the universe, and with the laws of nature and humankind. And, they hold court, when duty calls.

Keepers of Remembrance and Insight are our conjuring storytellers and translators who "just know" of things past and how they shape things present and future.

Keepers of Commerce are the business minds who bring about the checks and balances in our lives.

Keepers of the Cozy bring us warmth, softness, and nurturing. They grab hold and hug for no apparent reason. Then again, they always come at just the right moment. Always.

Keepers of the Chronicles are our life's missionaries and journalists who silently follow our progress and keep us in their prayers and meditations.

Keepers of the Assist are the "extra" hands on deck. They are our enthusiastic comrades who help get the job, large or small, done. They are the "just doers."

Keepers of Flame stand ready at the pilot light. They turn it up and bring it down . . . euphorically.

All are Keepers of our Lighthouses. They are our beacons, our sentinels, our heavenly and earth angels who wave the lantern and help to guide our way . . . on due course.

A family is much more than folks connected by blood. They are the people who we can depend on to make us laugh, soothe our hurts, and keep us focused. They also enter our lives at different phases of our journey. My extended family is . . .

Use the past to understand the circumstance, not to predict the future.

—Robin Johnson

The State of Grace

By Sobonfu Some

Let me begin by sharing some thoughts about the state of grace itself, about what people mean when they describe a person as living in a state of grace, and make a few observations about the expectation many people have that life will be, or ought to be, wonderful.

The state of grace is that holy and contented way of being that each of us strives for. It is that state, auspicious in the spiritual realm, in which we work out all our difficulties with care, and function peacefully in connection with other people in the flow of life. It involves progress in accomplishing the purpose for which we were born into the world, in a way that is pleasing to those around us. It is a state of devotion and integrity, of living harmoniously, of being looked at not as someone who is perfect, but as someone that others trust and respect. It implies a certain level of healthiness and psychological well-being.

The state of grace is not the same as success in any measurable way, nor is it reflected in social status. It is not determined by how much we resemble those whom many people admire. In fact, the person who has arrived at this state may not even be conscious of it.

Each of us passes in and out of this state many times in our life. This is a universal human experience. As we fall out of grace it looks and feels to us as if we are failing. Indeed we call it "failure"; a part of us dies. But this is the process by which we make space for the birth of something new, something more true to ourselves.

Something needs to be broken in order for a new state of grace to be born. It is the natural cycle of our spirit. In this way, we are born and die many times in life before we eventually return to the land of the ancestors. If we are going to achieve our purpose in life, we must be willing to fall out of grace and accept its lessons. When we feel righteous about ourselves, or deny our brokenness, we are fighting against the higher states of grace that await us.

Failure is built into grace. You cannot have one without the other. It's like two sides of a single coin. Everyone who has achieved a state of grace is certain at some point to fall, and to have fallen many times before. Every successful person, everyone you respect, will tell you that they have mountains of failure behind them.

Dealing with reversals is much easier in my village than it is here in the West. In the village you have people who are concerned about you and support you, knowing that their own happiness is dependent upon you. They also understand that failures are life-giving, that they are the engines of wisdom. Failures, they say there, come to show you that you are stagnant or wandering or that you have work to do.

Here is something I have been taught, and which I have had to learn over and over again through experience: To fall out of grace is a gift, one of the greatest gifts that one receives in life.

When we are in grace, we begin to take things for granted and we actually stop working on ourselves. Falling out of grace shakes us up. It reconnects us to the larger universe in order for us to see ourselves anew. It forces us to rediscover where our true center begins, and to learn what needs to be set aside.

Day by day, we work to maintain our state of grace. We do so not only as individuals, but also as a part of several interconnected circles of support. When we fail, the work of coming back into grace is something we cannot accomplish by ourselves; it requires the participation of others.

The cosmos, the universe, is the largest circle to which we belong. This is the realm of Spirit, of goddesses and gods, of our ancestors. The next circle comprises the planet we live on, Earth. This is the place of air, water, fire, soil, stones, and trees. Then comes our country and culture. Nearer to us is the circle of community, the friends and coworkers and others with whom we share our daily life. Our extended family makes up the next smaller circle, including our parents, children, brothers, sisters, uncles, and so forth. Lastly, I think of the circle of intimacy, which we share with a spouse or partner.

The role of all these different circles is to hold us in a certain place, in a certain way, so that we can flourish. When we are in a perfect state of grace, all these rings are functioning to support us, and even if one of these rings fails us, as they always do at some point, we have the others helping us. Our well-being can continue. It is when several of these circles, especially those closest to us, start to break, that we experience a fall from grace. As they fall apart, we can be left feeling entirely alone and abandoned. We are no longer able to bring our gifts forward.

The struggles we experience at different stages of our lives are mechanisms built into us that help us rise to a better place. They are invitations for us to appreciate life, to appreciate the good things left behind, to acknowledge the sources of our disappointment, and then to let go altogether in order to come back to grace. They rekindle the acceptance of self, of others, of the past and present, and they offer us the animating experience of being welcomed home and reembraced by the community.

For people in the village—and many other communities around the world, for that matter—it is a given that as an individual falls out of grace, so will the other members of the community because of our reliance on one another. Indigenous communities also know that, for the community to keep in touch with Spirit, this fall and rebirth of its members has to happen. Hence they push one another to take on new roles, to become adults, to become elders, or even to face death. They encourage one another to be swallowed by light, to let go of whatever comfort they are hanging on to and see that it is inadequate not to grow.

In the West, of course, it is so much different. Here the community will hardly ever support individuals who take a step off the cliff. To fall is disgraceful. There is, in fact, a fascination with suffering that is completely disconnected from the idea of growth. People do not see the goodness that grows out of failure. They immediately want to cut their connection with those who fall, and miss the point that the failures of others are also great teachers.

Knowing some of the rules of grace, for me at least, does not mean living with fewer struggles. I sometimes observe myself as an actress in a movie, and see that there is a part of me that does not really want to change. That is what happened when the elders asked me to leave the village and go to the West to share the ways of my people. I thought, "Wait a minute. I live so happily with everybody here. Why do I have to upset things? What is the point?" I crashed against the huge obstacle of my unwillingness to leave. Although I knew deep inside that it was necessary, I needed the community to push me, and to let me know that I either have to deliver my gifts or perish.

I wasn't sent to the West so that the village could be rid of me. In fact, I love the people there so much, and I thrive on their appreciation and the gifts I receive from them. However, it was necessary for me to leave this behind and be reborn in a new place, a place where I didn't know anybody, where my old world no longer existed for me. I never would have volunteered to do that. It was only the community's commitment to help me grow that made it possible for me to leave.

I have found that, in the West, the search for grace often takes the form of a search for ideals. "Who is ideal? Who is the best? How can I make myself like that person?" When the state of grace is understood as embodying an ideal, it can easily be turned into something distant and inaccessible.

In a world that has become individualized, fragmented and competitive, grace has become more of a challenge. When I think of how life once was in the village, I see there how community once existed in much of the world. People worked together at being in grace. It had nothing to do with being a leader, a hero, or a role model. You didn't need to be the king or the healer. Whether you were the person who lead, or gave medicine, or cooked, or hunted, or painted, or whatever—each person had a position within the community where a state of grace could be lived. You can still see remnants of such wisdom in the names people chose for themselves, and which many of us have inherited: Carpenter, Hunter, Miller, Smith, Cook.

The idea, "Every man for himself," has a cost attached to it. No one can afford so high a price.

I think there is a kind of selfishness that is nurtured by the economic system of the West. In Western society, there are so many opportunities for individuals to make big gains at the expense of the rest of the community. People will claim they have the right to do so. There are also certain religious dogmas that cause people to struggle with grace. Whatever religious tradition is dominant will affect the way you live, the way you think, the way you are judged. It's going to produce an umbrella of beliefs under which you are compelled to live whether you believe or not.

I have found in my work, for example, that where a certain, narrow kind of Christianity has been instilled, people accept that they have been born evil. This view infiltrates the way people look at each other: "We are all basically evil"; the battle against our nature never ends. This belief automatically limits a person's abilities to come back into grace. It's as if one's wings have been clipped before one can fly. It takes people out of the state of grace in which all babies naturally arrive.

For some, the dance between what we truly feel and what we have been taught, between our natural purity and narrow-mindedness, becomes a challenge. Perhaps this is one reason why some people have difficulty being with children. Children remind them of how far they have wandered from their natural state of grace, and, perhaps, of the obstacles they carry inside if they are to enter into grace again.

Look at children when they're born. They are in a genuine place that exudes laughter, love, freedom, and enlightenment. When you are with them, there is a vibration that makes everything peaceful. This is the state of grace where we all want to be—at one with everything, as a mystic might say—where there isn't separation, where there isn't confusion, and so forth.

The state of grace, of course, is not ours to hold on to so tightly.

Life happens. We all grow up. Moving from childhood to youth, from youth to adulthood, from adulthood to elderhood—each of these steps involves a kind of fall from which we have to rebuild ourselves.

Each of us has a stubborn conservative inside that steps out at times to stop us from progressing. You know, when everything seems to be working, why bother with wisdom all this stuff about growing?

We are all like children learning to walk: When we fall, we get up, brush off, and start over. Every time it requires determination, learning, growing, transformation, flexibility, and patience. These meditations suggest that the only way to remain in grace is not by learning to avoid failure, but by learning how to pull ourselves up after we fall.

Our Spirits Are Inextricably Entwined

By Mary-Frances Winters

No matter where we have been on our individual journeys on this
  earth
Or where we are going, we are One.

The beauty of our humanness comes from the breadth or our
  diversity.
The depth of our individuality and the wholeness and creative
  synergy comes
From the bringing together of each individual's special, God-sent
  gift.

The miracle rainbow that symbolizes our differences also shows
  us that when we are
Arched together in unison, we make a beautiful and lasting
  impression.

When we lift our voices in harmony, the resulting sound of each
   unique pitch creates
A melodious effect that no one voice is capable of.

We must find the loving spirit that dwells deep inside each of us,
That spirit which compels us to care, to serve, to share,
Which brings forth agape and provides the capacity for a change
   of heart.

We must come to a greater understanding of our connectedness.
We do not exist outside the universe.
We do not exist separate from other life forms, from other peo-
   ples of the world.

We must see the wisdom in creating new linkages—the power
   that emerges
From combining our energy as we strive to attain our universal
   vision.

A vision of respect for all humankind—a vision drawn from our
   interconnectedness
And enlightened by the spirit, mind, and body.

The Oneness of All

By Elder Emily Diane Gunter

From the Epilogue of
A Rite of Passage to Spiritual Enlightenment

I learned from the monks of Tibet during my trip to Himalayan Mountains that "a thousand arms and a thousand eyes of compassion" is an expression of unlimited love to all beings on earth. When you are compassionate to yourself, it is easier to be genuinely compassionate to others—unconditionally.

When you have not been compassionate to yourself and you show tenderness to others who do not return the compassion, you have an undercurrent of resentment toward them. You'll have a tendency to blame others. When you feel this way, stop, get quiet, and breathe. Continue breathing until you feel compassion and love for yourself.

To know God, you must go through your own Universal Heart with unconditional love, into the silence of your free will, bringing the loving light into your body. When you come out of this beautiful silence and interact with other human beings, your "thousand arms and thousand eyes of compassion" will be activated.

In practicing this unlimited love and compassion, each of us will joyfully comfort all those who cross our path. We also get to know and love God and obtain lasting peace. Be willing to breathe and relax and allow yourself to be compassionately loving to all beings, especially yourself. Anytime you need a spiritual lift, allow any of the following affirmations to fill your being, so that you may live in the Golden Age of Peace . . .

We are courteous, kind, and respectful in our verbal and nonverbal dialogues with loved ones.

Our jobs are carried out in the joy of being of service to others.

Our homes are sanctuaries of unlimited time and space where we feel the infinity of the universe as eternal, progressive beings.

Our bodies are filled with the warmth and nourishment of the Holy Breath of Purity.

We heal ourselves with the sweetness of the loving light of God through our hearts and to all who cross our path.

Spiritual and intellectual substance fulfills our desire to know the world we live in and all beings on it.

We desire to know the body we call our own.

We desire to truly know the soul and the wisdom whence it came.

We want to know truth, love, and balance in the loving light of God.

Our compassion gives us a true sense of social sympathy, that we are our brothers' and sisters' keepers. The continuity of our world is dependent upon that fact.

We all seek the comfort of life for all beings, especially the children who are among many of the poor and helpless.

Knowledge and education is for all beings, not just an exclusive few.

We touch every child that comes across our path with love and compassion.

As you journey on our path to spiritual enlightenment, close your eyes and open your spiritual eye. Feel all situations and people with your compassionate heart, and respond with your highest ego.

God is One. All of us are in God. God is in all of us. Therefore, we are One. As we grow spiritually in the Golden Age of Peace, acknowledge the Power of One. We can do many great things together as One Spirit. The spirit and comfort of God glues us together through our loving, compassionate hearts. Let us . . .

Pray together
Breath together
Sing together
Dance together
Applaud together
Be silent together
Swim together
Meditate together
Heal together
Love together

Love can solve all things. Believe. Trust. Heal. Live.

It helps us to grow when we let go of negative energy that we are harboring. Anger and bitterness stunt us and block our vision. A major goal in our lives should be to banish negativity and sweep out the seeds of despair so that we can be fruitful and prosper. I'm mending the fences in my life by . . .

Opening to Spirit

By Caroline Shola Arewa

The sky turned from grey to blue and the sun warmed my face. I sat quietly breathing in and *Opening to Spirit*. I wrote words of thanks in my journal as I recalled the blessings of the past few days in St. Kitts and Nevis, West Indies. I know that what we do not experience positively can only be experienced negatively. Therefore I try to release that which is not going well and focus on the radiance in my life, I had the opportunity to do both as I journeyed in St. Kitts and Nevis. In so doing, the creator showered forth blessings in abundance.

There was a wonderful sense on community as Sistahs and a few Brothas of the Diaspora joined together for the Caribbean retreat. People arrived for different reasons. I came to present a workshop on the healing power of the chakras, called "The Spiritual Woman." Many other workshops were offered on the same day. Throughout the workshops, the healing voice of Oya, the Yoruba Goddess of change, could be heard calling in the wind. During the few days we spent together, as the winds of change blew, I witnessed so much healing taking place both within myself and around me. I would like to share the words that found a resting place in my journal on a bless-ed Tuesday while I sat relaxing in my new friends' home in Nevis.

Nevis, 8 May 2001—from my Journal

I am a traveler. I have traveled. I entered the depths of the ocean in the Great Barrier Reef. I scaled the heights of the Himalayas in Nepal. I sailed the Nile in Egypt. On every continent I have placed my feet and shared my words. I have traveled inside and out. I know the depths of my being and the pain buried there along with my love, beauty, and passion. I know the heights of ecstasy, both in the arms of a lover and the stillness of myself. I know the calm of the river and its sensual flow. What I am saying is, I have lived, and many sweet memories have kissed my breast in this past week. This has been a most fulfilling week.

Never would I choose to travel for a week. No! I would want a year, six months, at least one month. When I received Maria Dowd's e-mail asking me to present at a workshop on the island of Nevis, I thought, "OK, I could make it, but only for a week?" Then, I went into the anticipated beauty of these rain forest–rich islands. As sixty others and I *Opened to Spirit*, time stood still. A portal in the earth opened and allowed us to explore the depths of our being. Together with the sea, air, sand, and sun, we played, laughed, cried, and healed.

Held in the arms of the ocean Yemonja, moved by the winds of Oya, supported by Ile, Goddess of the land and overlooked by Ra, God of the Sun. What a week. It was a loving experience, a healing experience, a forgiving experience. A touch of paradise dwelled both within and around us. It was uplifting to see Sistahs dance and smile, laugh and sing, embrace, learn, grow, and Be. A wonder-filled week that stands high as one of the most peaceful and fulfilling weeks in my life. It was so full, so rich, with new friendships made and nurtured. I can even say it was a year, six months, a month, a dream.

Give thanks and praises for the synergy that is created when we come together throughout the Diaspora and *Open to Spirit*.

Healing Images

By Queen Mutima Imani

Heal our Relationships with Earth and Community . . .

Visualize your community as healthy, whole, and vibrant.

Ask the spirits, the higher powers, to cooperate in healing the community.

Send loving energy (pink light) and healing energy (green light) to the community at a special time each day.

Create an altar that represents your love for the community.

Allow some time and find some space for communion with the earth. In communion, the earth speaks her language of quiet rhythms and you respond with quiet rhythms of appreciation.

Expand your love of self, family, friends, and community to love of all the peoples of the earth who share the journey of life.

Big Shoes and Pink Halos

By Maria Denise Dowd

My grandfather left this world on a breezy autumn day. My mother lost her father, my grandfather, my daughters' great-grandfather. He was ninety-one. He was a great, honest, God-loving man. He was perfect in my eyes. During his funeral on Monday, I watched and listened to four generations of family and friends rejoice in his glory, as he—Uncle Willie, my grandfather—had tenderly touched so many. My ninety-year-old grandmother continues to carry the family torch. She lives with Alzheimer's, but not woefully—not in the least bit. As we mourned, her humor amazed and calmed us.

On Monday, as I watched her emerge from the white limo, aided by her two youngest daughters—my Aunt Carol and my Aunt Jewel—the very first thing I saw was the pink halo that surrounded her head. My aunts had dressed her in a fine black-and-white wool suit and this magnificent black-and-white hat with a magenta-hued brim, and all I could say behind my smile was, "You go, Girl." I whispered in my Aunt Carol's ear, "Very good choice of hats." And, she quietly responded, "Yes, it makes a statement."

And, it did. Queen Mother—my mother's mother, my grandmother, my daughters' great-grandmother—had arrived to celebrate her husband's near-century-long life . . . and she brought along with her the splendor of this brilliant pink halo into the halls of New Creation Church. New Creation.

Scores of family proceeded behind her and her pink halo. And, she was led—in formation—by her white-gloved grandsons and great-grandson. I joined arms with my sisters—my expectant sister-in-law, Kim and my cousin, April, and I marched in my grandmother's footsteps. I held my head high in the cloud of my grandmother's pink halo, for I am her firstborn granddaughter—my grandfather's firstborn granddaughter—flanked by my unborn niece, Jordynn Sierra, and my grandparent's last-born granddaughter, maybe on this day not-so-ironically named the month of my birth. Teary-eyed, I breathed in the synergy and geometry of death and life. New Creation.

My grandfather's Spirit lives earnestly in me—his firstborn granddaughter and a very early riser, as he was. I believe that I walk pensively along his near-century-old cobbled road of high principles, resourcefulness, and thoughtfulness. And, when my day comes, I trust that he'll greet me with complete pride and joy, even though I never did get the secure civil service job he'd hoped for me.

His kiss to my cheek will be damp and his plaid flannel shirt will be musky. I'll meet him in his garden of mile-high collard greens and

Swiss chard. And he'll have a glass of sweet-as-can-be lemonade, made fresh by his strong, loving hands.

This writing is my morning meditation to my family, friends, and colleagues, as I step audaciously into my day—Blessed to walk in my grandfather's Big Shoes and in the radiance of my grandmother's Pink Halo.

Building Bridges

By Mary E. Paschall

Busy hands clap for Jesus, vibrations fill the air,
Moans of joy, moans of sorrow, sometimes in silent prayer,
When I think of Mt. Nebo, its fragrant pine needle path,
Trees and cousins aplenty, those memories make me laugh.

Busy hands churning butter, cooks everything from scratch,
Country sausage, fried apples, sweet oatmeal none could match,
I think of a country homestead with a sweet magnolia tree,
Warm cozy patchwork quilting, those memories strengthen me.

Busy hands create a poultice pungent strong medicine,
Red flannel warmth flowed freely, healed me from toe to chin,
Memories of Momma Celie's steaming spiked honey tea,
Still Angels linger watching, those memories comfort me.

Busy hands making biscuits, crochet scarves Argo stiff,
Cactus plants in red clay pots, create sharp pointed tips,

Memories of seeds and harvests, big families once strong,
Take me to the water, *those memories linger on.*

Busy hands peeling apples, tart slices, simmering sauce,
Steamy, hot sugared laughter, red-checkered tablecloth,
Strong bridges brought me over, times I just can't repeat,
But when my life tastes bitter, those memories are sweet.

Journey to Self-Awareness

I stand poised before my canvas,
I am Fearless.
I reflect upon Your Teachings,
I am Meditative.
I create the extraordinary,
I am Divinely Guided.
I am a vibrant work of sacred art,
I am Beautiful.
I portray the essence of Spirit,
I am Blessed.
I am Radiance, Love,
Grace, and Accord.

—Maria Denise Dowd

Silent Cry for Love

By Lois H. Carter

I remember crying silently in the backseat of my cousin's car. I was about sixteen. My older sister, my cousin, and I were coming back from a party. I remember being thankful for the darkness of the car so that they wouldn't notice my tears. I was crying was because I didn't think I was pretty like my sister and cousin. I've always been overweight and was very conscious of it. I didn't love myself and that feeling stayed with me for a long time.

I had no idea what to expect when I participated in a women's Rites of Passage workshop. It turned out to be a most rewarding experience. While the women I met were from all walks of life, within that weekend we became like sisters. I remember singing, "Am I my sister's keeper? Yes, I am!" with them and rejoicing in that fact. I felt the love and it was beautiful. A seed was planted within me that weekend. It was the beginning of a transformation for me, one that was completely unexpected.

Although I had a better idea of what to expect when I participated in the Rites of Passage again the following year, I was still in for a surprise. Both times were very amazing experiences but what became a part of me the first year, made the second time more special to me. The seed that had been planted was about to blossom. Although it was for only a couple of days, it truly felt like a journey. Our spiritual teacher's heart was so loving, it was as I'd know her all of my life. She gave me a gift that I always carry with me. She heard my silent cry for love, self-love. She told me that I was a queen, and by the end of that weekend I felt like one. This time around, deep in my soul, I believed it! For the first time in my life, I truly felt beautiful inside and out!

I remember gazing around the room at the different women dressed in white, waiting for our "crossing over" ceremony to begin. I saw how beautiful black women are in all our diverse colors, shapes, features and sizes. And I was one of them! I cried silently again . . . but this time it was for joy! And it wasn't about the outer beauty. We were all smiling and our inner glow radiated. We were queens and proud of it.

We were all given cards with angels on them at the end of the Rites of Passage ceremony. It was so fitting that the card I received was the Angel of Beauty. That weekend was the beginning of my journey to self-love. From that special day forward, whenever self-hatred rears its ugly head, I promptly remind myself, "I'm a queen." With that affirmation, I hold my head up and face the world as the beautiful black queen that I *know* I am.

Life is not an intellectual experience.

—Robin Johnson

I am limitless power;
My old perception of
Restrictions or boundaries
Are only illusions.

—Ona Brown

Mama Was a Magician

BY EDNA OLIVE

My Mama was a magician. Yes, that had to be it. In my unsophisticated, barely educated, and yet-to-be cluttered seven-year-old brain, there was no other logical explanation. It was 1967. And, it was the year I discovered I had a magician for a mother.

It's been said that God works in mysterious ways. On that day, I discovered there was something different and special about my Mama. This time, God was working through a chest cold. On the wondrous morning that changed my life forever, I woke up and realized I didn't feel well. So in my most sickly and pitiful voice, I told Mama I had a cold and that I couldn't possibly go to school.

I'm the youngest in my family and I always believed this position should've come with certain privileges that my older sister didn't have, such as being catered to when I was sick. But this particular privilege didn't seem to be in effect today. Instead of my Mama saying, "Okay, Little One, you can stay home," my hopes for staying under the covers dissolved when I heard the words, "Well, I can't stay home, your Daddy can't stay home, and your sister can't stay home, so you'll just have to go to work with me."

"Go to work with you?" I thought. "Didn't you hear me? The baby girl is sick! I need to stay home!"

But I knew Mama and nothing could change her mind. It never did. So in resentful silence, peppered with the occasional mumble under my breath about how unreasonable my Mama was being, I dragged myself through my morning routine. I washed up as I had been taught to, put on my clothes, made my bed, gave my teeth the usual quick brushing, snatched a few tissues out of the box for the trip in the car, and headed to work with a magician who happened to have me as a daughter.

As we pulled into the parking lot, my thoughts were filled with the boredom awaiting for me on the second floor in the room belonging to my Mama. I coughed my way into the office where Mama signed in every morning. I sighed my way up the stairs to Room 205, the place where I never suspected Mama worked her magic every day. I sniffled myself across the floor and plopped into the chair that matched the desk where, I soon discovered, Mama hid all kinds of secret magician things. And, in her typical fashion, Mama gave me a pencil, some paper, and a book and told me to read and write something to keep myself busy and, most importantly, quiet. So I dragged the pencil, the paper, and the book across the desk and began to quietly busy myself.

Early in the day I was so involved in entertaining myself and making sure I coughed at the right intervals, I didn't notice the magic. Kids came into the room and they seemed so much bigger and older than me. Some of them noticed my sitting at my Mama's desk and asked who I was. Mama told them I was her baby girl and that I was sick today but assured them they were going to do their work as usual. Some of them smiled at me and said "Hi," and I sneered back. After all, I was sick. Some of them were loud and engrossed in their adolescent whirlwinds. These kids didn't speak to me at all, but I sneered at them, too. Mostly, I just sat at the desk quiet and bored, with a drippy nose, reading and writing words neatly with my No. 2 pencil on the white paper with blue lines.

Swinging my legs back and forth from Mama's wooden chair with the wheels, I wished I were home under the covers. I didn't want to be bothered with these irritating kids my Mama had the dubious honor of interacting with. But even in the midst of my disgust with my current circumstances, I became aware that something magical was unfolding. Although the exact moment eluded me, the realization gradually descended upon me as the day progressed. *Something* special was happening. The children in Room 205 were changing and my Mama was the reason.

It all began with a look. As Mama walked around the room, I noticed that she was smiling. Then, I noticed that the kids were smiling back at her. And through all the smiling, the kids and Mama kept talking to each other the entire time. I don't think the room was ever totally silent. Instead, there was a constant, happy chatter. From my place at the wooden desk, I wondered what they were talking about and what they were all so happy about. After all, didn't they care? The baby girl was sick! They just kept talking and smiling and smiling and talking.

I asked myself, "What was Mama asking them?"

"Why were they smiling at her when she talked to them?"

"What were they saying to her that made her smile so much?"

There was so much smiling going on in the midst of my sniffles and coughs, I decided I'd better pay attention so I could get happy, too. So I put down my No. 2 pencil and pushed aside my white, blue-lined paper with all the neat words written on it. And I watched and listened.

Somehow I figured out that Mama and the kids were talking about a book. A book! That's what all the happiness was about? A book? Not that I had anything against books. I had dozens of books at home. Mama read to me all the time and we both loved it. But Mama didn't smile about any of my books like she was smiling now. And there definitely wasn't any giddy laughter like Mama had going with these kids. I began to worry. Perhaps they were doing something to please Mama I couldn't do, something that only much older and bigger kids could do. Then I realized they were reading the book to Mama. Reading? That's what all the excitement was about? They were happy about something as simple as reading? Heck, I could do that! My chest cold and my blue-lined paper all but forgotten, I decided to pay closer attention to see exactly what was happening between these smiling kids and my laughing Mama.

It went something like this:

Mama would ask a question and one of her students might mumble, "I don't know the answer. Ask someone else."

"Oh no," Mama would smile and say. "You know the answer."

Then Mama would give him some information or ask him to read the book a little more. Then, he'd read some more and suddenly, he'd blurt out the answer!

"Yes! I knew you could do it! You're right," Mama would declare. And he would actually smile back at her! He might even laugh with her! What in the world was going on in Room 205? I decided to watch some more. So I leaned forward across the big wooden desk and stretched as far as I could, so I wouldn't miss a single word.

Next, Mama would ask a girl, "Do you know what that word means?"

"Tell me what you think it means," she would whisper.

"I don't know, Mrs. O. Ask someone else to tell you," one girl shyly replied.

And Mama would say, "Oh yes, you do know what it means. Try reading the words around it and then guess at what it means in the sentence."

And the girl would read the entire sentence and tell Mama what the word meant! Then there would be more smiling and laughing!

Now I was really amazed! I was consumed with my discovery. My Mama knew how to perform these wonderful magic tricks with kids!

It was unconceivable to me to think my Mama could just give a kid a clue, and like magic—they knew stuff! What was going on?

From that moment forward, as I watched Mama work her strange and wonderful magic on the girls and boys who sat before her, I knew I wanted to do it, too. I *had* to do it, too. So, through a runny nose and a sore, dry throat, I accidentally and joyously discovered the thing that shaped my life from that day to this very day: My Mama was a magician and my Mama was a teacher.

Music to Our Ears, Lyrics for Our Creative Soul

By Maria Denise Dowd

Listen and you will hear
Her birdsong of synchronicity and rhythm.
Breathe and you will smell
Her flowers lay hands on rainbows.
Touch and you will feel
Her waters cavort with harmony.
Watch and you will witness
Her enchanting confections of
Sun, moon, planets, and stars . . .
In perfect accord with man and womankind.
Do you feel the vibrations of Her Spirit?

To know and assert your Spirit-guided creative self brings about a kind of joy that transcends all that is mundane and challenging in our lives. I can stake this claim because I, too, am a lifetime member of our Creator's magnificent concerto.

In God's melodic universe, we are born genetically imprinted to pursue our creative propensities. We recognize it, only when we open our eyes, ears, and hearts to the spectacular art of Nature.

This rhythm is made strikingly evident by the universe when feelings are stirred inside our souls, by merely watching a sunset or tide come in. Every waking (and sleeping) hour, God delivers our sheets of music. Are you opening to receiving?

She calls upon us to be a part of Her sweet, sweet symphony. However, She only presents Herself just below the bass line . . . then, she waits unwearyingly. She waits for humankind to engage in its litany of life's recitals. She waits for us to discover—at the appointed time and hopefully in *this* lifetime—our God-given vocations, then waits for us to begin our practice, and refine our workwomanship. Our Creator is our booking agent. She opens doors and presents opportunities.

But what do to many of us do? Instead of getting to work on our creations, we often are a "no show." We shun our rehearsals by taking the easy, low, or no road to death's end. Instead of making music, we allow the bows of dictates, mandates, laziness, fatigue, hostility, sorrow, or mania to overtake our artistic sensibilities. Rather than answering our Creator's calls to compose works of art or science, we decompose. We hear no music because we tune it out. Consequently, we ruefully sap the song out of our lives.

It's not God's intent for us to imitate, heckle, or nod our way through life. She calls for us to evict fear from the house (or, at least relegate it to the very last row), situate our creative energies on stage, and trust that She has taken the very best of box seats. When we follow our calling and do it wholeheartedly, She'll reassure us with encores, and She'll restring our hearts with faith. Our vocation is to embrace, not deny our or anyone else's lyrics. Then, sing praises to God.

Whether your creative calling is to bear children, fruit, music, conferences, civics, grassroots causes, a cure for cancer, or a mélange of many—know it, assert it, and be guided by Spirit.

I see the seedlings,
The newness of God Stuff
Growing before my eyes.
And, it fascinates me to no end,
No end in sight.
Only beginnings.

—Maria Denise Dowd

Cultural Shock

By Cheryl M. Cocroft-Noble

In Nineteen hundred ninety-seven, fresh from Milwaukee, full of
  enthusiasm,
I was introduced to another side of San Diego via the street
  people.
Young and old, white and black, male and female lying in the
  streets, one leg, no legs, using their salesmanship on me;
  teaching me how to deal with
  my own personal doubts. You should never give up!
I stared at first, not sure of what I saw, then I looked away, began
  to build a wall so I could go about my daily task of not becoming one of them.
Not only women street people, but also women in transition, had
  a special effect on me because I, too, am a woman, you see.
  Yes, one could knock on society's doors of plenty one too many
  times, sit down to rest from the pain of rejection, then say,

what the hell, I'm giving up.

My own consciousness is the key for me not to become one of them.

I am told that they are there for many reasons that could lead to homelessness. For new arrivals here,

there was only the YWCA available for women who had limited resources for a residence.

What did we do wrong along the way to get to this? Hotels and motels cater to wealth, which I do not manifest now.

But why are women and mothers, the image, the creatress— why is there no room in the inn for us? Has our labor of love, our toiling on the earth, our unselfish love been in vain?

From a home with multiple rooms to one room that is rented for months could be seen as a prison to some, a vacation for others—it depends on the circumstance.

A simple matter of a late check from whatever source could put you or me in the streets if you had no family or friends to rely upon.

Moreover, if you have not doctored on your self-worth and self-esteem—too many nos and negative outcomes may lead to your breaking point.

It seems to me we need to raise consciousness about this situation, because too many of us women are becoming a nameless, faceless "them" etching out a survival on the street.

52   Journey to Empowerment

I'm a Divine work of art and I'm proud of these qualities that I possess . . .

The Dark Night of My Soul Journey

By Rev. Victoria Lee-Owens

I first encountered my conscious destiny over twenty-five years ago, when I stood at what was a crossroad in my life, unaware that I had entered a place of dark journeying. I would either recover spiritually and physically from self-inflicted degradation or lose my life, not necessarily dying a human death, or remain in a zombie-ish state wandering bewilderingly through life. It would be an additional five years of drifting along as an unlearned parent to five children, after three failed marriages, the last one being of an abusive course, before realizing that I was emotionally still a child.

Looking back down that long winding road, I am grateful for the lessons learned and even the discovery that I was an alcoholic-addict. This sojourn actually saved me from sinking into a whirlpool of ignorance by giving me false courage to do that which I would not have been able to do under my own power. I went back to college and got my master's degree, yet something was still missing. I had no real concept of God except as the meanest of retaliators, because I was raised in a home where fire and brimstone were the rudiments of punishment for those things deemed not of God. Today, it's so wonderful to know that punishment comes by my own hands, based upon the choices I make. In other words, I am punished by my "miss takes" and less-than-best judgments, and not by my "testing the waters" to see how much can I get away with. However, in the fundamentalist belief system I grew up under, it seemed that everything was "wrong" in my youth. There was no fun, no makeup, no boyfriends, no movies, no sock hops or dances, no hanging out at the drive-in—the very lifelines of my peer group's world.

Eventually I found my first "Eskimo" in the person of a secret boyfriend, who guided me toward a way out of my depressed, repressed, and oppressed situation through the glow aroused by my first alcoholic drink. In that moment, I experienced my first "I don't care what's going on" feeling. In time, I found myself depending on liquid and powdery courage to satisfy that short-lived taste of euphoria. As it became less and less available to me, I sank deeper into the hold of addiction. Soon I would need a little "suppum suppum" just to make it through another day.

I recognize today, that I carried many of the characteristics of my mother (I still do, but I'm aware of them now, at least), whom I often thought wasn't equipped to be in this world. Little did I know that I was fighting the same deficiencies in my own life. The only difference was that I could mimic what I saw in others really well and, chameleon-like, I used this ability to mask my inadequacies. Eventually, it took increased usage of substances to engage *any* inner strength, this time to pick up my bed after a second divorce—and second set of children—and move forward in life.

Although I had been raised in a religious home and attended church frequently, I was never taught to rely upon the Divine Spirit or God that lived and dwelled within me, and to ask it to guide my way. Instead, I relied on that liquid courage to see me through the death of my father, whom I dearly love, and help me hold onto my anger toward him for abandoning me. I harbored feelings of deep sadness, rage, and lethargy, only to juxtapose them with hostility toward my mother. I'd ask, "Why hadn't she died instead of my beloved Daddy?" It would be years before I made amends to her and myself for thinking about my mother in that way. It took moving out of the country by way of military duty to journey back to self-forgiveness.

Liquid courage became my parent and I obeyed it for many years—through the last two years of senior high school, through college graduation and graduate school, into the military and into my profession as hospital administrator. However, through the fog of the late 1960s and entire 1970s, I caught glimpses of my call to service as a Religious Science spiritual therapist. I would eventually accept that call to my ministry. In the interim, I embarked on my journey to recovery.

Upon entering these programs, I detested having people tell me what to do, and my feelings were often hurt when I was told that I was unable to function properly due to my spiritual, emotional, and physical debility from intoxicants. I took it to mean that they did not approve of me or my behaviors, or perhaps that they were jealous because I'd traveled around the world, was earning a high salary, and outwardly appeared to be doing quite well in life. Paranoia set in, as I reasoned that people were conspiring against me. With time and growing willingness, I began listening to people who talked of knowing where I came from and the feelings that accompanied that state. I slowly began to recognize a sense of well-being through prayer. Was that a speck of light beginning to pierce through my dark journey?

Still unable to find any inner faith, a spiritual guide taught me how to sit and contemplate what God is to me, at least as much as I could understand about this new exercise called meditation. And what emerged was my vision of God as my very best friend, with no restrictions in that friendship. With continued seeking, through transcendental meditation and other practices that found me baptized, dunked, splashed, having hands laid upon me, and God knows what else, my course led me to recognize Infinite Spirit within. Today, there is a peaceful, spiritual satisfaction that resides in me, and with every step I bounce with the joy of knowing "I got over" to this side of belief. I'm now able to call upon it when darkness seeks me out from time to time. It delicately urges me to communicate with Divine Spirit and gratefully surrender to deeper clarity in my life. I practice being completely open to Divine Spirit by giving up that little egotistical part of myself that wants to hold on to patterns of negative thoughts and deeds. By retreating into meditation, I begin the process of complete abandonment to God's will, releasing my excessive imagination and selfish yearnings, and clearing the page of my mind for right and proper visioning.

While the universe conspires to give me just what I seek, from time to time inability overtakes me, sneaking in through a family trauma, hurtful words, through my adult children's behavior, or through people who seemingly ignore me. During these moments, I become agitated and agitating, unable to meditate. During these times, by connecting with spiritual practitioners and prayer partners, my strength is reclaimed. They help to anchor my intention to grow through that which darkens the night of my soul. The recovery is quick, as it's only a passing phase. And then, I'm made whole again, and am reminded of my need to always dwell in the protective shelter of unconditional love of myself and debunk all those strange, dark, senseless things.

I love the spaciousness of being whole and holy. Thank you, Spirit, for my deliverance.

Completely Out of the Box:
A Love Poem

By Maria, a Spoken Word Artist?

Create you own love poem, over and over and over again. Experiment with limitless blends of sights, touches, sounds, scents, breaths . . . And, propel your body poetry into cosmic motion, and know that it's safe to go to a wild, crazy, galactic place that takes you around the world and back again.

Let go and wrap everything you've got and take what you didn't know you had and allow your sacred self to stretch outside of the four sides of that pliable box with removable walls. Mold your parts in and out and around the body, mind, and spirit. Trust me. It will fit, like a loose goose that transports you to a heaven and back . . . and mighty tight-y, if that's your earthly pleasure.

Explore the prose in your toes, in the sand at the shore, and you'll discover that it only takes reading between the lines to reveal what's most sensational . . . to you. And, don't forget to study the seagulls that see high above and dive deep below to grab hold of what feeeeeeds them. Take time to learn what yearns, and yearn to learn about the cuckoo clock that makes your creative juices tick.

Ask and you just might receive . . . an original song, one that's solid gold and uniquely yours for show-and-tell. No secrets here. Talk it up and feel it out . . . on an open mic or in a haiku, that is. Because making love to your free-forming creativity is both artsy and aerodynamic. And, it feels oh so good doing it in the park or doing it after dark. Oh, yeah. Oh, yeah.

Know it, show it, bestow it . . . for your gifts glow like a sun and groove like a moon . . . full and blue and all like-a dat dat dat. Who knows, some time tonight, this morning or tomorrow afternoon you just might write a new verse for our ancient's love poem. And so, it is . . . and always will, or at least, always *should* be . . .

What I Weigh Is Not Who I Am

By Victoria Johnson

I was born in the segregated parts of the Deep South, one of eleven children. My brothers, sisters, and I worked in the fields of rural Louisiana, picking whatever crops were in season, while my father traveled north, for months at a time, earning a living as a farmworker. Once the harvest was complete, some of the men would pool their earnings and buy a used car that was barely able to take them back home; the men who could not afford the trip home would stay on indefinitely. It was always a relief to see my father walking down the road home, safe again.

Despite our poverty, our parents loved us deeply, and whenever we had money, family meals were a time of comfort and joy. When the crops were good, we'd feast on ham, biscuits with butter, mashed potatoes and gravy, sweet-potato pie and fried okra. We'd sit around the table for hours, talking and laughing. These special times were abundant and comforting.

When I was five, my parents relocated the family "up North" to Washington State so that my father could find more work and we children would have a chance at a good education in nonsegregated schools. I'll never forget the first day. As I peered into the classroom window, I was so nervous I felt sick. Here I was, one of four black children in the entire school, staring into a sea of white faces. The teacher tried to reassure me: "It's okay, Victoria. We're all the same, no matter what color our skin is."

Yet, I didn't see color. What I saw were little legs—pair after pair of skinny little legs. And my legs didn't look like that. Mine were big and round and they rubbed together when I walked. The teacher continued to try to coax me into the room. "They are just like you," she said. I wanted to scream, "They're not like me!" I have thighs and they don't! As I took my seat, which felt snug against my body, I realized for the first time in my life that I was different. I was big.

Despite every attempt to lose weight and be accepted by the other kids, I never outgrew my baby fat. By the time I reached high school, I was obsessed with food and dieting. As soon as I got up in the morning, I'd wonder what was for breakfast. Then, after the last bite of Mama's homemade biscuits and butter, I'd think about what she'd packed in my lunch.

By the time I went to college, one of my friends had taught me a handy technique for keeping weight off—throwing up. I spent a good portion of my college years hunched over a toilet and trying to hide my shame. Yet despite throwing up, I still managed to gain the freshman fifteen—and then some. Instead of paying attention to the signals my body was sending me—low energy, depression, and head-aches—I'd reach for a candy-bar pick-me-up or a jolt of soda with lots of caffeine.

You know the old saying, "If you want to look thinner, hang out with people bigger than you?" That's exactly what I did. To soothe my emotional needs, I hung out with women who looked like me, thought like me, and ate like me. Believe it or not, I was their fitness instructor at the time. Unfortunately, we didn't view exercise as a way to gain health—it was a justification to eat more. My girlfriends and I would get all dressed up in our workout clothes, barely break a sweat, and then hit a McDonald's drive-through. "Sure I'll have fries with that! I just worked out—I deserve it!"

One day while I was leading the class, I felt a little dizzy. Ten minutes into the workout, I fainted. The blackout scared me and I immediately scheduled a doctor's appointment. I sat with clipboard and pen in hand at the doctor's office as I began to lie about my health history, with no regrets.

"Has anyone in your family ever had diabetes?"

"No."

"Do you . . . ?"

"Nope, never. I eat fruit and vegetables and drink eight glasses of distilled water every day."

Then I had to answer the magical question, "How much do you weigh?"

Well, when exactly? In the morning? Before PMS? After PMS? I scribbled one hundred and thirty.

The nurse came in to check my vital signs and glanced over my questionnaire. "One hundred and thirty?!"

"Well, last time I checked it was."

"Please step on the scale."

"Shouldn't I take my shoes off? And my belt—it's metal; it must weigh a few pounds."

After removing everything I reasonably could, I stood on the scale, held my breath and pulled in my stomach, trying to be lighter.

She whizzed the metal bar way past 130 before she clicked to 150, 160, 170. When the ruler clicked at 175, I jumped off the scale in horror.

Still shell-shocked, I met with the doctor. What he said did little to soothe me.

"Young lady, if you do not change your eating habits and your lifestyle, you are on your way to developing type two diabetes." Holding a large syringe and getting right in my face, he continued, "You will have to take this needle and stick yourself with it every day. You will become a pharmaceutical drug addict if you don't make a major life change!"

His words hit me like a hammer. I thought about my aunt who had her leg amputated because of diabetes and my grandfather who had chronic heart disease. The doctor told me I was headed down that same path if I didn't do something . . . and soon.

After I left his office, I sat in my car and sobbed. A thunderstorm was kicking up outside—yet it was no match to the raging storm I felt inside. I had been given great opportunities in my life. My mother and father had sacrificed to provide me with an education and a life of equality. I felt like I'd failed to live up to their standards. And, I knew that I wasn't doing my life justice in this condition. Did I want to continue on the road to self-destruction or did I want to take control of my health? Did I want to be one hundred and seventy-five pounds and uncomfortable, or have a body that allowed me to move freely? Did I want to be out of breath and tired at the end of the day, or to have the energy to do things with my family and friends? I had to make a decision.

At that moment, I asked God to forgive me for not honoring the gift He had given me—the gift of life. I asked Him to forgive me for not honoring my body, my health, and my talents. I asked Him to please show me how to get well. I told Him that I promised to do whatever it took to do the right thing. As I prayed through my tears, something indescribable happened. I felt God's unconditional love. God promises us a "peace that surpasseth all understanding," and He'd given me a gift that day in the parking lot of my doctor's office. I suddenly felt freed from the prison of food addiction, poor health, and emotional bondage. I was enveloped by love and filled with a burning desire—a calling—to change my life from that moment on.

From that epiphany forward, I used the power of prayer and spirit to transform my existence. I turned my life over to Him, and He led me to people and places, books, and seminars that supported my transformation. I experienced a Body Revival. From that moment on, I dedicated myself to changing my spiritual life, my relationships, including my relationship with food, and my health. Step by step, each and every day, my life got better and better. I was shown a way to overcome my poor body image, my love of "comfort foods," and my old habits that had sent me down a road to self-destruction.

Once I overcame my own demons, I realized the purpose God had for me included service to others. In turn, I've had the opportunity to teach thousands of people how to fill the emptiness with something more than chips and soda.

Today, when I see myself on national television helping others achieve their victories, when I feel the rush of leading twenty thousand people to their "breakthrough" of self-defeating habits, or catch my reflection in the mirror training towering NBA basketball players on the importance of nutrition for their performance and career, I know that I've conquered the dark despair of secret eating, loneliness, and depression that I felt for so many years of my life forever.

Passionate and Purposeful Living

By Jewel Diamond Taylor

Sometimes your life may feel like a trip instead of a journey. Been there . . . done that. My life was a boring trip with one pit stop after another, looking for love, meaning, and my purpose. Some people go straight to their destination. They are born knowing what their purpose is. This revelation isn't always so obvious for some of us.

I took the long way. After working countless jobs, experiencing the learning and growing pain of marriage, loving and guiding my sons, wavering in my self-esteem, procrastinating and watching both of my parents close their eyes for eternal sleep, I finally accepted my purpose. Being a conduit of hope, motivation, and encouragement in a nontraditional way was my destiny. When I finally told the truth to myself and took my leaps of faith to develop my gift and purpose, the spark inside of me became a flame of passion.

Once I had found my passion and my purpose, I began to discover a tenacity, self-motivation, creativity, faith, and resilience that I had never tapped into before. Because of my passion to speak, teach, enlighten, and serve, I began to make investments of my time, money, and faith. I became emotionally invested and rooted, and nothing and no one could stop me. Passion put me on automatic pilot toward my goal of being self-employed and a forerunner in the motivational/personal development movement. Even though there were detours, financial lean times, and lonely days and frustrating moments, my passion never diminished.

Over the years, I've had a lot of car drama—"bad Carma." Years ago, my car was repossessed. Another time, my transmission dropped out of a car on the way to one of my seminars. I had three flat tires on the way to another seminar, yet I kept going. Years ago, I had a car totaled in an accident on the way to taping one of my cable TV shows. I got a ride and kept going. I've presented workshops when I was very sick and had to face major surgery. Over the years, I have been invited to speak for no money, little money, and late money.

When you have a passion that is your j-o-y and not a j-o-b, you don't become discouraged easily. When your family is your passion, you find ways to be, do, and give even though it seems like, looks like, and feels like there is nothing left to give. Passion is a fire with you that keeps you going when everyone else says its too crazy, too hard, too far, too late, too much, too risky, too giving, too old, too young, and too expensive. My passion for life, for family, and for my purpose and career path has pulled me through self-pity and depression. Passion doesn't give or accept excuses. I pray to God daily to allow me to keep my passion lit.

I know that life offers joy and pain, sunshine and rain. And I know that my passion allows me to endure the pain and down times in life. My passion is my inner alarm clock to get up even when my body is tired or in pain. My passion pushes me to make one more phone call, or take one more vitamin to stay healthy, or to get up and walk or practice my yoga to reduce physical stress. My passion pushes me to smile instead of cry. It pushes me to keep going even when I feel unappreciated, overlooked, overworked, or over-whelmed. My passion empowers me to speak up and PUSH (Push Until Something Happens).

Several years ago, I realized that I could share my passion by teaching a seminar, "Do You Have a J-O-B or a J-O-Y?" I sincerely believe that once you discover and embrace your purpose and stick with it, the pursuit will become your passion. I've seen it demonstrated time and time again. You can turn your passion into your profession.

Passion is your fire in your belly, heart, and soul. Passion is an inner fire that burns away any procrastination, fear, indecision, or worry. Passion doesn't sweat the small stuff. Passion keeps you self-motivated. Passion gives you a reason to keep going when everything and everyone else says stop, or wait, or why are you doing that? Passion gives your life purpose. Passion is what gets you up in the morning and it will keep you up at night when others are sleeping. You rise to the occasion because passion can pull you through your pain, self-pity, self-defeat, depression, and sorrow.

A Season of Reinvention

By Kamili Bell

I am going through a season of reinvention. I have not yet discovered who it is that I am about to become, but I am well on my way. The journey and this season of limbo are at time confusing, yet delightful. One thing is for sure—I am not the same girl that I was four years ago, or even last year. At both times I was involved with two different people, neither of whom I imagined myself actually being with, yet both of whom I lied to and told many wonderful, sweet things they wanted to hear.

I said these things because I was neither strong enough nor brave enough to tell the truth, and I needed their acceptance. Without it, how would I know I existed? It was so much easier to lie, both to them and to myself. I wasted so many years pretending. I am not that girl anymore. Right there and right now in this new space that I am in, I know that I am smart, beautiful and funny. I no longer seek external approval or affirmation of who I am.

My inability to love myself honestly and openly stemmed from my experiences of a very tormented childhood among my peers. For reasons I have never been able to pin down, kids my own age just didn't seem to understand or like me much. Inclusion in the "rat pack" was all I ever wanted! As a result, I spent many years trying to change my face to adjust to whatever crowd was newly listed as "in." I never allowed myself a moment's truth because I believed just being "me" wasn't good enough. It would never gain me the acceptance I so desperately thought I needed. At times in my life, "me" could've been just about anybody at any given moment, and was always subject to change. Such a life is exhausting. All I really wanted was a sense of belonging without the compelling need to make changes and adjustments. No matter what wonderful things my mother, my grandmother, or my aunts told me about myself, I was incapable of believing any of it. How on earth could they know these things about me if I had no clue?

These feelings of inadequacy, of being a misfit, carried over into my adult life. But I put on a smiling face and figured none would be the wiser. Suddenly, I became this person that everyone just loved and clamored to be friends with—always smiling, always laughing, always ready for a good time. Even though this was exactly the external acceptance I'd spent most of my years in search of, I just couldn't trust it. I thought I was smart, funny, and worthy of acceptance, but I never really believed it. As a defense mechanism, I surrounded myself with an impenetrable wall. I painted it with the pretense of being too complex to ever really be known, but I never gave anyone a chance to know me, including myself. I coated it with ambivalence and pretended not to have the energy to engage meaningfully in relationships, platonic or romantic. The truth was, and is, I'm just dying to let all those walls down, and to be completely honest without fear of the vulnerability honesty can create. I no longer feel the need to prove who I am or justify my existence to anyone, which is a step in the right direction. I am who I am.

Who am I? I'm still that little weird kid who likes to bury her nose in a juicy book rather than go to loud parties; listens to relatively unknown bands rather than the radio play list; likes digging though the racks of Goodwill more than shopping at the mall and loves lazy days spent in the company of a few very good girlfriends. I still have a ridiculous sense of humor that causes me to let loose uproarious laughter at any given moment. I'm no longer afraid or ashamed to be that kid.

Who am I? I am bright, intelligent, and full of laughter. Who am I? I am vulnerable and no longer afraid to admit it. I am not a stone wall; I am not as strong as the rock of Gibraltar. I am naked to the world, yet my spirit is strong. I know I am marvelous—not because anyone else says so, but because it is true, and I believe it. Of course, hearing it is great. But I no longer need to hear it. To depend on the outside is counterproductive and will only inhibit my ability to love and know myself.

I can let go of my fear of betrayal and admit my vulnerability. I

Journey to Empowerment

can be honest with others and myself, and I recognize that the consequences will not be painful but rather invigorating.

I am going through a season of reinvention. The journey is at times confusing, yet always delightful.

I Looked into Her Eyes

By Eleanor Ballard-Gadson

I looked into her eyes, and the sadness I saw was heart wrenching. I tried to reach out to her with my eyes to let her know, that I understood what she was going through.

She gazed at me for a moment, and seemed to nod as if she understood my concerns, as she continued to be the victim of his insults.

She stood every bit of five foot four and he was at least six foot two. He looked down at her as he told her what he was and was not going to do for her.

She had a child in her arms, one in a carriage, and two stood on either side of her. It was their father's face that they had and it looked as if he had given birth to each of them himself.

I sat helpless staring at her, while he continued to browbeat her with his words. She looked up at me once again and with my eyes I tried to communicate my thoughts to her. Stay strong. Take care of you. Don't let him hurt you. It won't last forever.

She gave me a faint smile as my train pulled out of the station, and I wept in silence, for she reminded me of my past.

She was me a long, time ago.

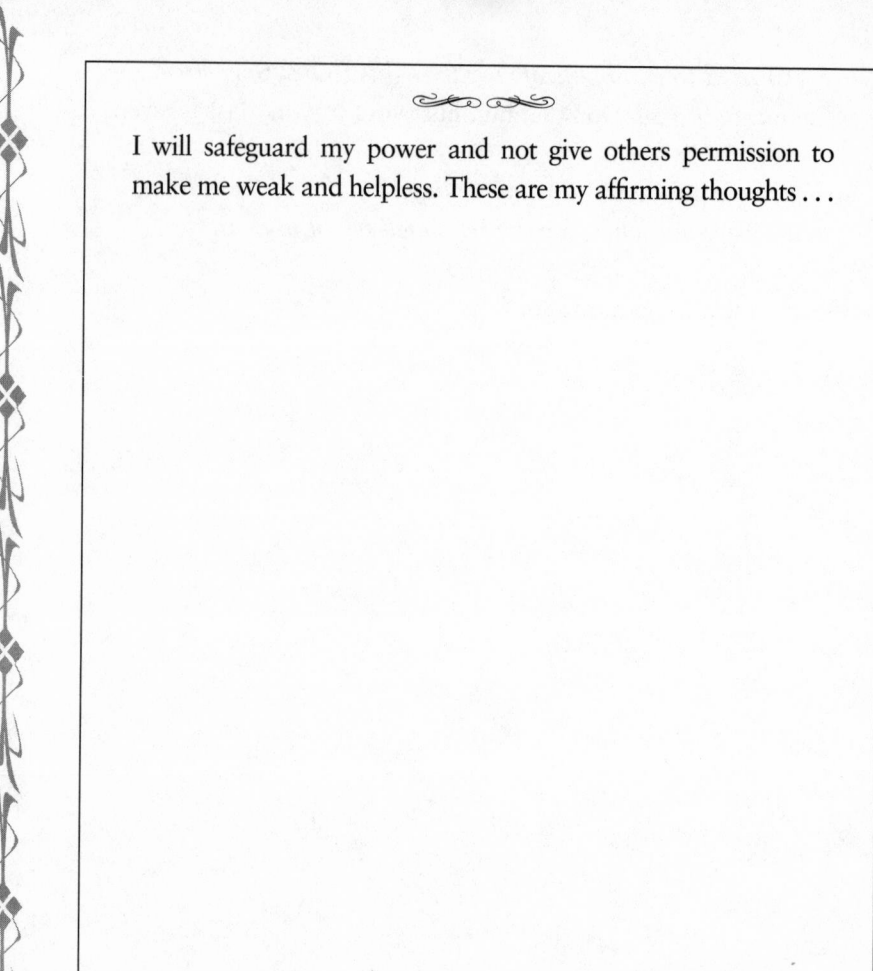

I will safeguard my power and not give others permission to make me weak and helpless. These are my affirming thoughts . . .

Journey to Womanhood

I fully love myself in shadow and in light.

—Queen Mutima Imani

In Honor of Our Elders: Wisdom Along the Way

By Shikana Temille Porter, Ph.D.

"An Elder is more than a prophet."
—Ga proverb

My wisdom-purposed journey towards womanhood commenced a little over ten years after the landmark Brown v. Board of Education decision. In the beginning, there was a second grade teacher, Mrs. McClain, a tall, slender African-American woman with brown-sugar skin and who wore black horn-rimmed glasses. She was gentle, kind, and smiled as if she really liked us. It was Mrs. McClain who determined that my best friend, Rachelle (another cute little chocolate child), John (a chubby, cheerful Asian boy who loved to stretch out his arms and pretend he was an airplane), and I were to be assigned to the mentally gifted minors (MGM) program. Being placed in this category would lay the foundation for an educational path marked with enrichment, even though I often felt guilty because we were set apart from the other children. It did not seem fair that a different learning style determined who would be destined to less intellectually stimulating classes.

Then there was a fourth grade teacher, my favorite teacher, who taught with passion, creativity, and style. She, too, was tall, played the guitar, and taught us how to use chopsticks. When I was nine years old and five feet, six inches in height, it helped to have a role model who stood three inches above me and said out loud that it was "beautiful to be tall!" Mrs. Knudsen conveyed much respect for me and reinforced my love for learning. She had speed-writing contests and my new best friend Lisa came in second to me every time. At the end of that school year, Mrs. Knudsen predicted that I would become the editor of *Ebony* magazine. These wisdom-based moments at a school "high on a hill by the mountains, far above the sea . . ." left an indelible mark on me.

On another significant pathway, there was a professor, my favorite professor, Dr. Danny L. Scarborough, who insisted that I call him Danny. Every lecture was a perfectly choreographed experience with drama, class, and deep knowledge. He pierced my soul with introductions to poetic renderings from Mari Evans and Maya Angelou.

My development as an African-descended woman was shaped by the power of Nommo (a Swahili term referring to the generative and productive power of the spoken word) experienced in that classroom. When Mari Evans came in person to read from her book, *I Am a Black Woman*, my dramatic interpretations were vigorously enhanced. Furthermore, Danny captivated me with his profound expressions and visions. He insisted that Zora Neale Hurston wearing a red hat had come into the room when I entered and took my seat. One day after a glance in the mirror, briefly, I saw her too! What a lesson in how to speak possibilities into the lives of young adults who deep inside believe empowerment is their destiny and simply need cues to help them claim it.

Now, as I reflect on the impact of my examples of excellence in early childhood and post-secondary education, it is easy to see their influence on my teaching philosophy and approach. In each scenario, there were wisdom seeds planted in those lessons that would eventually blossom when the time was right. Mrs. McClain, Mrs. Knudsen, and Dr. Scarborough were foundational figures in helping to foster my personal and professional growth. Clearly, they spoke with hope and truth about who I was and yet to become.

Certainly, this early grounding would sustain me in the ensuing season of harsh criticisms and judgments that seemed to color my graduate school experience. In fact, it was the remembrance of being identified as "gifted" in elementary school and the African-centered framework in the Department of African-American Studies at the university I attended that would help to remove doubts about my ability to pursue a doctorate in clinical psychology. In particular, Dr. Shirley Weber, Dr. Shirley Thomas, and Dr. Norman Chambers provided a rich, culturally centered context that would later serve to enhance my practice as a psychologist. For them, and what they shared, I remain eternally grateful.

Although I haven't published a magazine article yet, *Ebony* is still a possibility. Indeed, I am not a cultural anthropologist. However, much like Zora, my love for writing, inquiry, and the desire to connect past, present, and future are ever so strong. When I teach, I seek to inspire, reach, and engage students in the manner that my Elders did. Even though a good foundation for teaching was in place, it surprised me that having a passion for the discipline, respect for students, and a love for learning would not be enough.

Right before the start of graduate school, my childhood friend and I returned to our elementary school to see Mrs. Knudsen. She still remembered us and was happy to hear of our achievements. Years later, after giving my card to her cousin at our twentieth high school reunion, Mrs. Knudsen sent me a postcard full of positive praises. It's amazing how good that still feels and so much of what has unfolded is because of what she poured into my life.

It is in the blending of public scrutiny and praise that we find a way to our true centers even though both can seemingly be unbearable at times. Teaching has taught me not to take myself so seriously and that if I disregard the worst and the most glowing evaluations, a realistic assessment of my performance will be more possible to attain.

My hardest lessons taught and learned were in the courses that attempted to challenge my movement beyond rhetorical multicultural content and right into the heart of diversity matters. Whether it was

Ethics, Introduction to Psychotherapy, The Psychology of Women, or Multicultural Issues in Psychology, there remained four constant core threads. My very presence assured that race, class, gender, and culture were woven into the tapestry of each classroom encounter. Depending on one's viewpoint, intricate patterns would begin to emerge and captivate imaginations, or some would remain distracted by the tattered strings and knots on the other side.

Sometimes it seems impossible to get to the deep thoughts that penetrate and linger, as Danny seemed so capable of doing consistently and with ease. One day in particular, I found it painfully hard to engage in any meaningful dialogue beyond a superficial level. Aside from dealing with viral flu residuals, I just could not muster up enough strength to say what needed to be said around racism and feminism—two themes that the students chose to react to on that day. It began with one woman insisting that white women are oppressed in the same manner in which women of color experience. She cited examples of discrimination, rejection, and degradations to make her point. My immediate reaction was a defensive one and initially thwarted any attempts to facilitate discussion. My challenge was to convey how oppression is manifested differently. Fortunately, I recalled another wisdom-inspired moment that occurred while team-teaching a Cultural Diversity course with Dr. Oliva Espin. She put it best: "One cannot *not* have privilege." We were then able to explore the idea that with privilege comes a responsibility to act in a way that uses it proactively and productively. Her words created a nice shift to empowering possibilities, rather than comparing oppressions.

Whether we are in or outside of the classroom, we carry with us what we remember. What we remember and choose to share can make a difference in the lives of children, youths, and young adults who are open and trusting of the process. Truly, when the students are ready, willing, and able to find their rightful place in life-changing discourse, while acquiring wisdom along the way, every divinely appointed Elder-teacher-learner will appear.

Call to Ritual

By Maria Denise Dowd

It's been a long day, my Sweetness. Let's connect—although it's late—for a moment, perhaps over a shared jumbo mug of mint tea infused with raw honey, Honey. We'll talk through the steam and share glimpses of our day past and our plans for tomorrow and the day after.

Maybe we'll spit a sweet orange, ripped from its skin and handed from my lips to yours. We'll savor the citrusy zest that tingle our mouths wanting more.

Shall we soak in a warm bath scented with ginger or jasmine or lavender? And, fill the room with candles and the kind of music we love to love by and by? In short order, the multisensory-surround-us-with-gentle-taps pulsate the epicenter of our blended hearts. This time, you'll rest against me as I massage your scalp, and tug at your earlobes and remind you of all the things you already know about yourself and us—my king, your queen, our kingdom. Playfully, you splash water—properly anointed—on my cinnamon-ness and we watch it bead onto your chocolate-ness, then into a pool of bliss. What a luscious thing we have.

Perhaps . . . just for fun, you'll shave my legs. You *know* how antsy I get about stubble. You'll glide your thumb along the inside curve of my slender foot and I'll wiggle my copper-painted toes because your kisses tickle so.

Our home is a bit chilly on this night, so we'll bustle our buttered nakedness to into our bed, and like an army of veteran soldiers . . . left . . . left . . . left right left . . . our limps intertwine in perfect formation. Who will light these candles? I'll defer to you, cuz you can take the heat of the cold better than me. But, I'll keep your side warm, and witness the first cast of glow against my curves and your straight lines. You'll return to a waiting, wanting me . . . and we'll caress our Divinity.

I'm no longer chilly because we feel our skin to skin because we love the skin we're in and how our skins blend . . . infinitely. Oh, what a blessing you are to me . . . and me to you.

Good night . . . or perhaps good morning by now.

Shall We, My Sweet?

By Kali Ashtar

Shall we, My Sweet?
Yeah, go 'head . . .
Enjoy the decadent, dark and gooey.
Make me wanna go . . . ummmmm . . . Uh hum.
Yummy for my Honey Tummy.
My-eye King of thee Supreme Elixir . . .
Me, you, our lickety treats . . . Oh, yeah . . .
Just wanna stink my tongue into . . .
And, whhhhirl until my honey tummy aches . . .
For your morning you.
Oh . . . jeez . . . my tasty treat.
Banquet for a Goddess . . .
Feast for a Warrior Priest.
A Fete . . . grandly, lusciously fashioned.
Your syrup oh so thick . . . and delicious.
All up in my pores,
All up in my/your open door . . .

To the grand room of passion hearts,
And other lip-smackin' morsels.
For your eyes and taste buds only.
Spoon me up, lick the bowl.
This Honey Be yours to eat . . .
A nibble here/there . . . li'l tang with a bang.
Engulfed all over the place.
Raw, Raw Honey . . .
Black 'n' Strapped Molasses . . .
Naturally Nectar . . . So Naturally So.

The blessings and grace that have been bestowed upon me leaves me amazed. I that thankful for . . .

Plights of Passage

By Maria Denise Dowd

Therapists know. Physicians know. Prison administrators know. Spiritual healers know. Drug and alcohol rehab counselors know. We all know someone who knows.

No, I don't *know* the precise statistics, but I'm certain that we'd all be floored if we did. However, people in the healing and empowerment business have worked with enough people and have garnered enough knowledge and insight on just how devastating sexual abuse committed against our children—and, primarily our daughters—has been to the black community. Much of our rates of obesity, alcoholism, depression, drug abuse, promiscuity, prostitution, imprisonment, relationship and sexual disorders and dysfunction can be attributed to this single root cause—sexual abuse. And, from what we've likely witnessed amongst family members and sisterfriends, these kinds of wounds don't always heal with the neatness of a skinned knee. As sure as one has forgiven, the experience is surely not forgotten. Thus, "getting on with your life" may not be such an easy proposition, especially when we've continually dismissed the ordeals as commonplace.

"Well, that's life." (According to whose laws of morality and humanity?)

"If I got over it, so can you." (Is this the whole truth, and nothing but the truth?)

"It could have been worse." (Says who?)

"Ain't no female safe. That's just the way it is." (So, no one is responsible for protecting the other half of the world's population?)

How has it happened that so many of our children's rites of passage into man-and womanhood have been at merciless, fouled hands of pedophiles, rapists, or sexual harassers? How has it happened that we have been so engrossed in our own busy-ness, fear and pride, that we haven't seen our children's anxieties and anguish? How is it that we can put the onus on our daughters to keep their "skirts down and panties up," when someone much older, more trusted, and certainly more coy might be testing their innocence? This is not a "blame 'n' shame" crusade. However, we must talk about it to fully comprehend it . . . and its far-reaching consequences, when left ignored and the pieces disconnected. Let's consider the aftermath of the aches—most often subconsciously borne—passed on to next generations.

We have to talk about the warning signs. And there *are* always warning signs, if we're paying attention. A grown woman can conceal an abusive encounter. Children are not so ingenious. Even when they might not shed tears, there are signs that cry for help, and those signs are usually so commonly textbook, they're like cold, hard slaps in the face. We must not presume that our children "act out" because they are bad or are "naturally" quiet or withdrawn. Children don't plummet out of the blue. We need to protect our children's bodies, minds, and souls, and not concern ourselves with creating "embarrassing situations" or financial hardships. Our children come into our world pure and wholly reliant on us for their safety and well-being. Know than the damage could be irreversible and those demons could follow them to their graves, but first not without many days and nights of living in the hell of the memories. Your assumptions about "survival" rates and probabilities don't matter. No child deserves to be force-fed this kind of anguish.

And, women who've been victimized need to talk about it—both to help and heal. Forget nasty little family secrets, promises, and hurt feelings. By talking about it, we can hopefully lift the burdens and possible save a child from a similar fate.

We need to keep a brow raised to all of the people our children and teens come in contact with. Let's not sensationalize it. Most child predators don't lurk in bushes and dark alleyways. They sleep in our beds, sit at our dinner tables, baby-sit, borrow sugar from across the fence, and take our children on outings. They could be our husbands, boyfriends, fathers, brothers, uncles, cousins, grandfathers, neighbors, and close friends of the family. Most are men. Some are women. While some might assault without warning, most will take the time with our children to build trust and even love. Look closer into our children's eyes. Watch their interactions with and reactions to the people in their lives. We do the laundry; check it. We tuck them in at night; talk. Teach them the differences between "good" love and "bad" love. Then show them "good love" regularly and unconditionally. Assure them—through words and actions—that you love them and want them safe. Watch, listen . . . and never betray their trust in you.

We need to remove our rose-colored glasses and see things as they are—within our homes, schools, churches, and other places where our children are presumed safe and secure. We need to share our stories of "plights of passage" so that we might save our village's children from similar fates.

What moves me to tears is when others give their power to someone else who then makes them feel insecure and insignificant. I resolve to remain self-assured and independent by . . .

Ivy Reid

By Nancy Lee

Motherless herself at fifteen, my mother's journey was multifaceted. She immigrated to the United States from Jamaica having been coerced into marriage by another immigrant from home who played her fears of being a single woman in a strange, hostile country, of facing the world alone, of making a life by herself in the so-called Promised Land. There may have been some attraction, but her decision to marry my father probably was based mostly on fear.

In the States, her income came from what I see so many of our people doing today caring for white people's children. Her articulate husband managed to snag a position as a law clerk until he was let go after the 1929 stock market crash. His new position as an elevator operator required long hours and enough endurance to face racism in all its demeaning dimensions. He was a proud, intelligent man who wore the mask of fake gratitude and fake cordiality while smothering real anger and the very real fear of not being able to adequately provide for his burgeoning family.

Always resilient and resourceful, Mom proposed getting a Harlem brownstone to convert into a rooming house. She would go to work using her newly gained skills as a seamstress while he managed the property. Proud and chauvinistic as he was, my father would have none of it. He wanted to return to Jamaica where he already owned land. She balked, but he insisted and eventually took the children back home without her. The separation lasted seven years until he became ill, and she was forced to return to Jamaica.

What she encountered when she arrived was a mortally ill husband who had been diagnosed with rapidly advancing cancer, but rumor had it that a jealous brother-in-law had poisoned him. Dreams of good life in the Promised Land had faded into a bleak reality. Before my father succumbed to his fate, he impregnated my mother one last time and passed away two months before I was born. I look back from my adult perch and wonder how she endured; I doubt I could have.

I came out of the womb too soon. My older sister had had trouble in birth, too, and suffered irreparable brain damage, so she was never the true self her personality suggested—a friendly, outgoing foil for mother's nature would allow her to take care of the physical needs of her children with great skill while turning on us with a mighty tongue that could rip our self-esteem to shreds. We all felt it differently.

Newly widowed, my mother single-handedly brought her three children from the island to the States—one bewilderingly different, a heartbreakingly handsome and burdensome son, and a premature newborn. Back in Harlem, relatives provided shelter as she continued her journey to independence. A hard-won tenement apartment with rooms to let provided a way of making an extra buck for herself and her three children.

In our cold tenement apartment, my mother would listen to her baby girl crying and pleading to be let into her bed for comfort and solace; meanwhile, she needed that comfort and solace herself. Blessings from God and a diligent, watchful mother kept the apartment from catching fire from the oil stove we used for a little heat. Oh, the stress and broken sleep it must have caused.

My mother's only son, and substitute husband, would provide the catalyst for escaping the tenement with the GI Bill he'd earned after a stint in the U.S. Army. Mother had saved her pennies to make the down payment on a two-family Cape Cod home. We had made it to the Middle Class.

Her journey lasted ninety years. A proud and strong woman to the end, she died from a hospital mistake that left her helpless against a medication that completely cut off her circulation. While her death was unfair, her sacrifice provided for her children and her grandchildren who would share the proceeds from the sale of that two-family Cape Cod.

When we retrace our ancestral heritage, it gives us the courage to go on because the nature of things tells us that their journey was usually more difficult than our own. We have the choice to embrace it, to learn from it, to be in awe of it or perhaps to deny it.

My mother was so many things, fulfilled so many roles—mother, breadwinner, matriarch, teacher, disciplinarian, and role model.

Star Angel

By Carmen Cassandra Crews

Dedicated to Yvonne Crews

I always said,
"If God ever put one of His angels on earth—then it had to be
you."
You always have time to talk, to listen, to understand
With all of your own that you have to do.
I don't have enough breath in my body
To say how beautiful you are
And when I think of you—my heart smiles
Needless to say, you're my Shining Star.
Mom, you are my saving grace.
When you reach out, it's always to give
Even when I don't deserve,
You make life happy to live.
All that you mean to me,
What's a girl to do
Except fall to her knees
And thank God for you.

Queen Mother

BY CARMEN CASSANDRA CREWS

Silver Nappy Hair
Sparkle Diamond Eyes
Ocean Pearl Teeth
Ruby Red Heart
Black Leather Skin
Cotton Spirit within
Sapphire Soles
. . . A Story to Be Told . . .
About Mother
About Queen Mother
About African Queen Mother
About Beautiful African Queen Mother
About You
About Me

We must love to appreciate our own unique beauty and not let others define or belittle our characteristics. I love being me unconditionally because . . .

Writing Ourselves Back to Strength: Part II

By Jackee Holder

Okay, so I'm a writer, and you think that all of this might be easy for someone like me. Think again. So many times I found the very act of putting pen to paper extremely challenging. It has been recently that I have been able to honor the writer woman inside me. The proceeding years of constantly turning up on the blank page in my journal cleared the space so that she could live.

I'm feeling really cozy now as I sink myself into the words I am sharing with you. My mind is wandering as I ponder about the relationship between the fingers that hold the pen, the ink inside the pen, the blood that flows through the fingertips, the hand that embodies them and the connection to the heart.

The blood in our hands and the ink in our pens are blood sisters. The energy of their juices creates chemistry on the page that is saturated with our truths. How divine that hands which palmists tell us have our lives written all over them guide the pen across the page. Our thoughts may start in our minds, but our hearts are really their authentic resting-places. Once there, they become our truths. Hence, the theory of "blood sisters," whose lifetime oath is to take us as close to our authentic selves as possible. The hand is truly holy: on the hand is the finger upon which we place a ring as a declaration of love; the hand is the first to touch a baby's head as she makes her entrance into the world telling her she is safe; and the soothing touch of the hand comforts someone in pain. How can such a holy vessel lie? Though the hand we will eventually humble ourselves as we write. As the words of Proverbs 18:4 share, "A person's words can be a source of wisdom, deep as the ocean, fresh as flowering stream."

We humble ourselves as we write. What do we find out about ourselves? This is the question I am seeking to unearth as I plow though the words on this page. What I accept the fullness and the potential of my life and all our lives, I know that there are no edges to our worlds. Woven into the lines and loops of our words are the imprints of our deepest and innermost desires, and it is our hand that leads us there.

I am of African ancestry, born to Caribbean parents who migrated to England, where I was born and raised. The sheer expansiveness of the journey traveled so I could be here permits me to have no boundaries on where I can go or what I can desire for myself. The African in me longs to live by the sea, to go to sleep with the sound of waves in my ears, and to rise knowing she does not sleep. It is my journal that safely hears me tell of these desires. My hand coaxes these truth, pulsating from the womb of my birth, speaking to me of the things I can't easily reveal in public, like how I long to make love in the open, naked by the sea. When all is said and done, the lover in me is also the mother in me; she is the sister and the friend, the aunt and God-mother, the woman speaking at the podium, a body moving through the aisles of the market, a thousand different faces all wrapped up in one, all with their own secret desires. My journal knows them all so well.

Sometimes our lives hit a spot that scares the living daylights out of us. It really does feel like the lights in our world have been switched off. I hit that place several years ago as I watched a seemingly successful career collapse around me, and I retreated from the world. I was wise enough to consciously take time out to be with myself. While being with myself, I realized how much I had been missing the real me. A period with very little money in these times can send even the most sane of us mad. I felt inadequate and found myself sinking deeper and deeper into a place of desolation from which I wasn't sure I would return. Even when surrounded by people, I felt alone. My journal through these times was my constant companion. She stayed with me, witnessing my thought and my moods, and gracefully allowed me time to wallow on the page in self-pity. I know that these lean times are often the periods many of us find the most difficult in which to write, but it is the most crucial time for the journal writing to continue. It is during these times that we are writing ourselves back to wellness, health, and strength. I had to keep on writing to live.

Journey to Empowerment

Most of us on the spiritual path will not escape the barrenness of the wilderness experience that when explored beyond that surface contains an oasis of healing and magic. It does not discriminate against whom it will claim. I have found it to be the most disturbing yet the most fascination part of my journey. It has been scary, yet it has been the greatest place of my healing. It is the dark dawn before sunrise. Had it not been for the journal, I would have wobbled over and sank deep beyond the shores.

The wilderness is where your Goddess takes retreat and runs with the wolves. It's where she lets her hair down, has little or no responsibility, and can do and be just whomever she pleases to be. We must capture her on the page so we can reclaim aspects of ourselves seemingly lost. As you write through your wilderness, your hand will guide you to a sacred well inside of you where you will embark on a journey of the world. Here, in the darkness, your words will dig the trench to find water so you can drink your life back into being. Here, as you continue your excavation, you will discard and release the internal chains that have held you prisoner and your words will guide you home. The woman who runs with the wolves and who can see herself in full flight on the page is a woman who someday soon will not be afraid to live with all of whom she is. The ancients knew that the wilderness was a place of spiritual cleansing and healing; a place to move closer to authentic self.

I am happiest when I am writing or curled up reading a book.

Women who attend my workshops often comment on not being able to find time in their busy lives to write. One part of me responds silently, "Then you don't have time to live.' The more compassionate side of me has another response, "Seven minutes of spiritual grace it all it takes."

My birth chart number is seven. Seven, energetically as a number, is charges with a sacred energy. The seventh day has been initiated into the rhythms of the Earth as a Holy day, the Sabbath day, the day of rest. I am very connected to the number seven and its sacred charge. One day, as I wrote in my journal, the following inspiration flowed onto the page—what if every day we committed to take seven minutes to embrace Spirit in our lives? By practicing this myself, I was amazed at how grace appeared—sometimes softly and other times boldly as I wrote in my journal for seven minutes or went for my morning run in the park with my pocket-size journal in tow.

I took this inspiration into one of the workshops I run, "Connecting with the Goddess Within." I simply guided the whole group to spend seven minutes in silence completing a journal-writing ritual. The group was presented with three questions probing into the deeper self and encouraged to write without stopping for seven minutes. The goal is to write past the internal critic and to write right into the center of the authentic soul. This was a place of honesty, and Spirit always honors the honest soul. The results for many were profound. Afterwards, they shared the experience with each other, and the air in the room was electric. I affirmed that day that all it takes is seven minutes of spiritual grace to remember your spirit and nourish your soul.

Since then, I have been preaching the virtues of the gift of seven minutes of spiritual grace. My goal is to perform my seven minutes every day because, when I do, it sets my heart on fire. The mind can cope with a goal or an intention in bite-sized chunks. The secret in taking seven minutes is that you naturally end up spending more time than the original seven minutes you set for yourself.

I have taken the seven minutes beyond the ritual of journal writing. Some days, I spend seven minutes working on a collage for my new journal. On another day, it will be seven minutes spent staring out of my kitchen window across miles of London skyline. Or then again, it may be seven minutes arranging a bunch of flowers in a vase and soaking in the beauty of Mother Nature. The possibilities are endless, but whatever you do will a sign for amazing Grace to step right on in.

So here we are, nearing the end of our journey together. I simply invite you to take seven minutes each day to be with your journal, to be with your spirit and to be with your soul. Sarah Ban Breathnach in her book, *Something More*, said of women of power, "Life needs women who will claim their power, and will use it for all of us." I believe that writing for our lives is a healing tool that will guide each one of us back home to the center of our soul where we can reclaim not only our authentic selves but be fully connected to our soul's purpose.

I pray that we as African women around the world will continue to weave together the pieces of our fragmented selves from among the words on the page and piece them back together again like our grandmothers and their mothers before them who made the beautiful quilts often depicting the courageous stories of their lives. In doing so, we nurse ourselves back to strength, to our original glory, celebrating the enormity of who we are. As we welcome both the sun and the rain, the thorns and the flowers of life, we keep faith and keep on stepping out, holding on to the vision to just be—all that is WOMAN! In the meantime, sisterfriend, don't forget, you are the best things you've got!

Be blessed.

Take a few moments each day to find your center. Give your mind the opportunity to relax and reflect on your abundance of blessings. When I'm centered I meditate upon . . .

The Day I Told the Truth

BY SHELLIE R. WARREN

I'm a liar . . . in recovery.

Ever since I can remember, I've lied. Sure, I guess we all have at one time or another. We've lied about eating the cookie before dinner, about taking a glance at a fellow classmate's schoolwork, about being seventeen when a cute twenty-one-year-old approached us for our number. These are called "little white lies"—the ones we say will hurt no one. But these fabrications only set the foundation for bigger ones, the kind I have told and have paid the price for.

"I don't need a serious commitment."

"I am comfortable with casual sex."

"I prefer 'nonrelationship' relationships."

"I'm too young to know what I want in a relationship."

"Sharing my needs is a sign of insecurity."

"Putting a man's needs ahead of mine is all a part of compromise in a successful relationship."

"There's no way I can keep a man without having sex with him."

Lies! Lies! Lies!

And, the sad part is . . . I had come to believe them.

I've been in many destructive relationships with great men. The men in my life were highly intelligent, very humorous, and keenly attractive. They were all goal-oriented and ambitious. And, many of them were candidates for healthy, productive relationships . . . that is, until I started lying to them, but never without first lying to myself. You see, I had many friends who sent the men in their lives through unnecessary drama. They were jealous and possessive. Many of my male friends complained about the high level of maintenance that dating young women entailed. Thus, I pledged to be unique. I was determined to mold myself into the ideal woman, the kind of woman men desired.

I would be attractive and intelligent and funny and would want no more than what a man was able to give. I would not demand a monogamous relationship or have "unreasonable" expectations, for that would surely put unnecessary pressure on them. I would listen to all of their female issues and would provide the solutions. I wasn't going to be the stereotypical "typical woman."

However, over time, I not longer felt attractive or intelligent and had started to lose my sense of humor. What I discovered, over time, was an intense longing for a monogamous relationship. But, after years of living this way of life, how could I turn back? Or, why should I? At least this way I was not vulnerable to the men that I was involved with. How could I be? They were in my life on *my* terms. I was receiving the benefits of being someone's girlfriend, but without the responsibilities. I had it made! That is until they started ending their relationships with me to be with the very women who "didn't understand" them. But, I thought that *I* was the understanding one!

To the contrary, I'd been lying to myself and they'd been lying to me. My relationships were built upon falsehoods and denials. I was not the cure, but the Band-Aid. Sure, they wanted me in their lives, but as a diversion or vacation. I wasn't considered the main, the only woman. Then, I began demanding to be. But, it came too late. When they ended it, I was hurt and lonely. I felt cheap and used. While sex had distracted me from my pain, it was something I no longer enjoyed. What had the potential of being healthy friendships, ended as toxic relationships. I disliked them for not loving me and they did not trust me enough to learn how. I was now addicted to this way of living and it was causing me to die at a slow and steady emotional death.

One day, it dawned on me. My problem was my lying. So, my solution had to be to tell the truth.

"I am attractive."

"I am not a doormat."

"When I am not honest with a man about what I want in a relationship, I cannot blame anyone else but myself."

And the biggest revelation of all was, "I AM A QUEEN!"

And, "Queens deserve no less than kings."

The day I came to know these truths was one of the scariest, yet most exhilarating moments in my life. I knew that in order for me to live free of self-affliction, I had to give up the drug that once provided so much comfort and relief for me—self-deception and incongruity. No more convincing myself that my heart and body should be taken casually. No more inviting low expectations from men. No more mistaking lust for love. No more camouflaging piercing, ardent pain with temporary, carnal pleasure. I deserved much more. And, what I wanted was a monogamous, moral, upstanding, permanent relationship first with myself, then with others.

I'm freeing myself from the secrets of my past, and I'm excited about my future. I am thankful that God granted me the opportunity to come into this revelation. Relieved that I can do nothing about yesterday, I'm grateful for a chance to change tomorrow. But mostly, I'm appreciative for today . . . a day that will be filled with no lies.

Only truth.

She Sings

VALERIE AYRES

She sings off-key. But, wears her voice like the beautiful family quilt her grandmother stitched one corner at a time. It was an heirloom pattern; colorful but never out of style . . . loud but not overbearing. Stitched beside the wood stove that the family used for heat and cooking everyday meals. Her granddaddy named that stove Betsy. It was black, potbellied, short, and heavy, but don't let looks fool you 'cause it could heat up the whole house in a matter of minutes with a little help and simmer up meals that had you licking each finger twice. "Just like Miss Betsy," the menfolks whispered to each other. Her voice not one to gossip with such foolishness, instead sings chords full of life in radiant spring hues like her family quilt to family, friends and neighbors alike . . . always in key.

She sings off-key. But, wears a piano like a second skin and plays like she's been taking lessons since birth; plays by ear with a gift only God could have given her. After hearing the first stanza of a song, she will pick it apart key by key and make it her own. She first will stroke the ivories like brushing a baby's head and, by mid-song, she will bam out the chords as if it is being twirled towards the welcoming sun all the way from her soul. You, the listener will walk away feeling the heat, shaking your head wondering where she hid the sheet music and how someone with all that class could hit those church keys that hard with so much rhythm, find all that soul in such an angelic place and conjure up all that power from such a petite package. You smile as you walk away a little lighter realizing how blessed she just made you feel and how good God is . . . all the time.

She sings off-key. But, wears the beauty of a note like a lost soul that has just found joy on its way home. A note that you hold for a long time as it relishes on your tongue and after it has left your soul, you try to hit it again . . . and again . . . and find pleasure in knowing that once you hit it, it will come back, sometimes more forceful and longer than before. It will bring passion and beauty like a ballad with words written just for you and a melody played so sweetly with so much profoundness it brings satisfaction to your heart and tears to your eyes. She takes that note every first Sunday and sings front and center as a member of the seniors' choir, soprano section. Even though her voice leans more toward alto or tenor depending on whom you ask and what note she is trying to hit at that given moment . . . she still sings. With so much wisdom, she goes where the spirit leads her and

where she feels her voice is needed the most . . . amazing grace. . . .
She sings, to us all.

She openeth her mouth with wisdom; and in her tongue is the law of kindness.
 —Proverbs 31:26

Mine Own

GEQUETA VALENTINE

After twenty-two long hours, she lay stretched out on a bulky metal hospital bed, exhausted and disoriented, her body soaked with the perspiration of hard labor.

"It's a girl," the white nurse had said, without enthusiasm, moments after the child, kicking urgently against her loins, emerged from her womb. After checking the baby's vital signs, the disdainful nurse cleaned and wrapped her tightly in starched white hospital linen and hurriedly handed the bundle to her without speaking another word. Protectively, she held the child in her trembling arms, while the newborn flexed her young vocal chords with a deafening cry, announcing her presence to a world that did not want her.

She stared at the small black body, pressed closely against her bosom, silently mourning the inevitable. For all of the joys she would experience through motherhood, she knew that the baby girl would suffer much more sorrow than even *she* could ever imagine. But the woman could not allow those thoughts to stifle her spirits. What she had done was give life to yet another yearning, black child and for that she was proud, even content, and that was what she needed to remain focused on; not the fact that far too soon she would be forced to reconcile her emotions and confront the reality that this very child would be yanked from her care, just like all of the others, into a world that refused to understand her. She would be thrust into a world already set in motion, entrenched in its own ideologies about whom or what she could and could not be.

Why had the woman been chosen to bear such a burden? Wasn't it enough that she'd survived the same? To teach another, was harder to do. No matter how much she'd prepared them all, it just wasn't enough to soften the blow to the barrier she'd erected, always broken by a single word or action.

Her daughters would run to her like their lives depended upon it, shocked and amazed that she already knew and felt their pain, even before they had arrived. She consoled and encouraged, all in the same breath, her smile never wavering, while her insides were ripped to shreds at the rejection her children suffered. Each time, more dreadful than the last, having given each child a portion of her own heart for her healing, to cover the scar that the scorn of others had left. Even now as she gazed into the deep brown eyes of the child she held, she felt as if she had nothing left to give.

Her eyes trailed the room to the open window, for a glimpse of the great big world outside, a world that had changed, but not enough that she could allow her children to play in it without questioning the age-old adage that "every man is created equal."

"Run faster."

"Try harder."

"You have to be better," she would exhort them while they stared at her, eyes filled with naïveté, never understanding why they were held to a higher standard in the first place. But they were and would continue to be, by no fault of their own. It was just their plight, as it was hers to nurture and strengthen them for endurance. Without it, there would be no way that they could survive.

For that reason alone, she knew there was no point in continuing to tussle with her thoughts. No sense in debating what was already determined. She had been chosen, appointed to bear such a burden, and she could not shirk the responsibility, no matter how daunting. Heartache and agony, never far away, peeked at her from every corner, always prepared to stop and pay a visit. But if she dwelt on what was always a possibility, she would never remember the rewards garnered by her dutiful service.

The familiar sounds of hunger erupting from her child's mouth brought her back to her surroundings. Looking down, she smiled, gently nudging the squirming infant, guiding its mouth to her darkened nipple. As it nestled and suckled her, she was happy for the job that she'd been given, of being her mother, and the mother to the entire nation of children she'd borne before her. It was her job and hers alone. To ask someone else to do it would have been unfair. The task rested upon her shoulders. And yes, the weight of it bent her frame every now and then, but who better suited to raise her daughters to be proud black women—who love and believe in themselves in the midst of a world that whispers their inferiority, but her . . .

A black woman.

Heavenly Body

By Lyndon Harrison

I look upon thee as a flower looks upon the sun,
You . . . are my heavenly body.
I rise to meet you at the dawn of each new day,
Looking forward into the light that your vision brings.
I see all of creation in a single of your gestures.
No greater honor can I hold than the touch of your divinity.
Angelic being, as your heavenly essence descends deep into my
*   soul, I am blessed.*

Our energy motions attract like the elements of an atom.
Deep in our emotions . . . we feel our way home.
We are on a crystal-clear path . . . traveling through the darkness
*   and the light.*
But no diamond could lure me from the perfect gems hidden in
*   just one of your tears.*
For only we, the stars and our creator can know the truth about
*   our homeland.*

A place of profound beauty . . . where we were once one.
Separated by an age to test our love.
Unified in this way to complete the ultimate love story.
Light of the world . . . our union is indeed.

Your ra-pose makes me sigh the secret breath of bliss.
The most essential acknowledgement of love and respect.
As I open and close the lens of my central eye your image is
  captured forever.
On full display in my private gallery—the holy of holies.
Only you may enter this highest height altar.
Now your view of my entire being is unrestricted—I am yours.

Signs of the times . . . we are icons of fertility and stability.
Heavenly bodies decorated with the blueprints of raw life,
Our obits are free in form.
The first binary star of a new universe of galaxies . . . of worlds to
  be born.
Through the twilight eye light of our beloved ancient guardians
Our creator honors our ascension.
They prepare the way as the debris of universal construction
  implodes.
Our explosive union is visible to the naked eye.

Blessed is the place where we live.
Constantly moving in prayer, I give thanks . . . constantly.
Angelic woman . . . my heavenly body.
Only the most divine word can truly express our love.
A sacred word hidden in the spirit of our bodacious dancing and
  stillness.
Born wild and free . . . we have . . . returned.
My sweetest, mother of the purest creation, I love you.

Menopause/Womenopause

By Patricia Wilson-Cone

The dictionary tells us that menopause is the cessation of menstruation. My first concern is, why do we call this phase of women's lives *menopause*? Since we are talking about a pause—stop—a halt in the lives of women, it would seem to me we would change the name to "Womenopause."

We, women of color have learned since slavery the importance of pausing and stopping during the various stages of our lives in order to survive. We had to pause and stop when we saw our black men being castrated; we paused and stopped when we gave birth to the master's child; we paused and stopped when our husbands left us in order for him to survive in a land of freedom. And, now we journey into this biological phase of our lives and realize that a change is coming over us. Once again, we find ourselves pausing and stopping to embrace menopause, or what I have termed "Womenopause."

I want to define menopause—"Womenopause"—from a spiritual perspective. This is the time in women's lives when we should pause to reflect, revisit, and reshape our thinking; refine what we are feeling; remember where we have come from and where we are going as strong women of color; womanist creatures of God. This is a time where we want to be sensitive to the change that is occurring in our lives, and to realize and affirm that God is right there. It is the essence of Psalm 139:7–10. "Womenopause" might cause you to feel that God is not there with you. However, God is right there in the midst of our change.

This is the time to reflect on some of the outstanding African-American women of our lives and what they have offered us to enhance our spirituality. For example, what is Renitta Weems saying to us at this time in our lives as we read her book, *For Such a Time as This*? What does it mean to pause and reflect on Susan Taylor's book, *Living in the Spirit*? When we feel melancholic during this "Womenopause" experience, dare we to spend time revisiting Maya Angelou's poem, "And Still I Rise."

It would seem to me that "Womenopause" would afford us the opportunity to reflect on the importance of what God says: "Be still and know that I am God" (Psalm 46:10). This is the time for women to just "BE." Be the woman God has created you to be. This is the time to "BE" the mother to your children at a slower pace now; "BE" the wife to your husband, and reflect on how you can creatively reshape your marriage. If you are single, "BE" the single woman, "BE" the single mother, "BE" attuned to the single self-hood, as you move in new directions with a newfound soulness. There may be times during

"Womenopause" when you may feel down and out, all alone or lonely. This is the time to call that woman or women in your life, so that they may build a circle around you and empower you with the spiritual light of perseverance. In this circle, experience God in the center of the circle. The circle concept is not strange to us, women of color. We know that the women in Africa encircle themselves as they listen and tell stories to one another. This is the time to come together with women in the church, on the job, in the sorority, in the community, in the shopping center, in the family and so on, and talk about the menopause, "Womenopause" experience. When we tell our stories, we women can become more liberated. Yes, there is a balm in Gilead, and it makes me whole as I journey through "Womenopause."

This is also the time to pause and name what is going on inside, then call out these various experiences to God and invite God to hear our prayer. During "Womenopause," we thirst for water; we find ourselves thirsty and sweaty about our brows. And, in the midst of darkness, we find ourselves changing our bed linens and night garments. But, there is another kind of thirst; we find it in Psalm 42:2: "My soul thirsts for God, the living God." Praying or crying out to God in the midst of our distress can fulfill this thirst.

We can pause, stop, reflect, revisit, and reshape our relationship with God, by praying. Prayer causes us to develop a higher relationship with God; in prayer, we rethink some of our petitions and intercessions with God; prayer causes us to thank and praise God for our womanist experiences. This prayerful relationship with God affirms that, yes, our bodies are experiencing a biological cessation according to our developmental stages as women. But the good news! God never ceases in our lives, no matter what our "Womenopause" experiences are.

> *Most Gracious and Loving God,*
> *Please empower we women to take time today*
> *To do all that you have called us to do.*
> *Let us take the time to be women . . . and pause,*
> *In the light of our day-to-day circumstances.*
> *High One, give us the courage to be empowered.*

There are some things in this world that I cannot change, situations that are beyond my control. Instead of wallowing in unhappiness, I will accept the challenge and not let it tear down my spirit. What will be, will simply be . . .

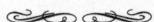

My magnificence exudes the happiness and positive energy that I bring forth. These are my empowering thoughts . . .

Today I soar and am thrilled about these incidents that enrich my life . . .